32

W9-DEV-038

EMPIRE OF THE AZTECS

GREAT EMPIRES OF THE PAST

GREAT EMPIRES OF THE PAST

EMPIRE OF THE AZTECS

BARBARA A. SOMERVILL

LOUISE M. BURKHART, HISTORICAL CONSULTANT

CHELSEA HOUSE
PUBLISHERS
An imprint of Infobase Publishing

Great Empires of the Past: Empire of the Aztecs

Chelsea House
An imprint of Infobase Publishing
132 West 31st Street
New York NY 10001

Library of Congress Cataloging-in-Publication Data
Somervill, Barbara A.
 Empire of the Aztecs / Barbara A. Somervill.
   p. cm.—(Great empires of the past)
 Includes bibliographical references and index.
 ISBN 978-1-60413-149-9 (acid-free paper) 1. Aztecs—Juvenile literature. 2. Aztecs—Social life and customs—Juvenile literature. I. Title. II. Series.

 F1219.73.S657 2009
 972'.018—dc22

                    2009016715

Chelsea House books are available at special discounts when purchased in bulk quantities for businesses, associations, institutions, or sales promotions. Please call our Special Sales Department in New York at (212) 967-8800 or (800) 322-8755.

You can find Chelsea House on the World Wide Web at http://www.chelseahouse.com

Produced by the Shoreline Publishing Group LLC
Editorial Director: James Buckley Jr.
Series Editor: Beth Adelman
Text design by Annie O'Donnell
Cover design by Alicia Post
Composition by Mary Susan Ryan-Flynn
Cover printed by Bang Printing, Brainerd, MN
Book printed and bound by Bang Printing, Brainerd, MN
Date printed: November 2009

Printed in the United States of America

10 9 8 7 6 5 4 3 2 1

This book is printed on acid-free paper.

All links and Web addresses were checked and verified to be correct at the time of publication. Because of the dynamic nature of the Web, some addresses and links may have changed since publication and may no longer be valid.

CONTENTS

INTRODUCTION

MORE THAN 20,000 YEARS AGO, THE LAND THAT IS NOW called Mexico was a rugged wilderness. The climate was cooler, and the land was rich and fertile. Rivers cut through valleys. They filled lakes or poured into the Pacific Ocean to the west or the Gulf of Mexico to the east.

A region in central Mexico stretched south through modern-day Guatemala and Honduras. Today, that area is called Mesoamerica (the word means "middle America"). Over many centuries, distinct groups of people lived in Mesoamerica and developed great cultures. They included the Maya, the Olmecs, the Toltecs, and the Mixtecs. (A culture is the religious, social, and artistic beliefs and customs of a group of people.) Starting in the 14th century, a people who called themselves the Mexica created the last of the great Mesoamerican cultures. The Mexica are better known in history as the Aztecs, and the lands they ruled in central Mexico made up the Aztec Empire.

The Aztecs did not dominate huge areas of land, as did other great ancient empire-builders, such as the Romans and the Persians. But, like the Romans and Persians and others who created empires, the Aztecs united different peoples under their rule. They created wealth for themselves by taking tribute from the peoples they and their allies conquered. (Tribute is something of value paid by one state to another as proof of loyalty or obedience, or to secure peace or protection.) The Aztecs controlled their empire for more than 100 years. Only the invasion of the Spanish, beginning in 1519, ended their rule.

7

CONNECTIONS

What Are Connections?

Throughout this book, and all the books in the Great Empires of the Past series, there are Connections boxes. They point out ideas, inventions, art, food, customs, and more from this empire that are still part of the world today. Nations and cultures in remote history can seem far away from the present day, but these connections demonstrate how our everyday lives have been shaped by the peoples of the past.

How Is It Pronounced?

Chichimec:
   CHEE-chee-mehk
Huitzilopochtli:
   hweet-see-loh-
   POHCH-tlee
Mexica:
   meh-SHEE-kuh
Mixtec:
   MEESH-tek
Quetzalcoatl:
   keht-sahl-KOH-ahtl
Tenochca:
   teh-NOHCH-kuh
Teotihuacan:
   tay-oh-tee-HWAH-
   kahn
Texcoco:
   tesh-KOH-ko

FROM UNKNOWN ORIGINS

No one knows the true origins of the Aztec people. Legend claims that Huitzilopochtli, the patron god of the Aztecs, gave the people their original name—Mexica. (A patron god is one who is honored as the protector of a particular people, place, or thing.) Only the myths of the Aztecs remain to tell us where they came from and how they began.

The tale begins in Aztlan, the legendary first home of the Aztecs. The name means "place of the herons" in Nahuatl, the language of the Aztecs and other nearby peoples. The Aztec legends say that in Aztlan, seven tribes lived in seven caves. The tribes were the Acolhua, Tepanecs, Xochimilca, Tlalhuica, Tlaxcalans, Chalca, and Aztecs. Together, all these people were known as the Chichimec. They were hunter-gatherers and lived a simple existence. Hunter-gatherers are people who hunt game animals, fish, and gather wild fruit, roots, nuts, and berries to feed themselves. They spent most of their time searching for food.

At some point, the first six tribes left the caves. But the land where they settled became extremely dry and suffered from a long drought (a prolonged period with no rain). As food became more difficult to find, the tribes had no choice but to leave. Eventually, they settled in the Valley of Mexico. This was not a joint venture, however. The six individual tribes traveled in search of six separate homes. Each tribe established its own culture.

The Aztecs did not leave with the others. They stayed behind waiting for a message from their gods, who would tell them when to leave. Some 300 years later, an eagle came to rest near the Aztecs' cave and cried out, "Let us go." The people took this as a sign that it was finally time for them to leave. Other Aztec legends say that it was the god Huitzilopochtli who told the people to leave.

The Aztecs left Aztlan in about 1100. They became nomads—wandering people with no permanent home—and had very little luck in finding a good place to settle. For a time, they found a temporary home at Tula, the city of the Toltecs. At that point, the Toltec civilization was declining. As the last of the Toltecs followed their king-priest, Huemac, in leaving their capital, the Aztecs moved on, as well.

Having left one great but ruined city, the Aztecs arrived in another great city that had also been abandoned. This was Teotihuacan, known as the home of the gods (although it had been built by the Olmecs). The Aztecs were impressed by the two great pyramids and the temple to the god Quetzalcoatl. They studied the paintings on the walls that told them the story of the people who had once lived in Teotihuacan.

SQUATTERS IN THE VALLEY OF MEXICO

Finally, after traveling for more than 100 years, the Aztecs arrived in the Valley of Mexico around 1195. They were the last of the Chichimec to reach that fertile valley. The Valley of Mexico was big enough to provide land and food for all seven tribes. But by the time the Aztecs arrived, the best land was already taken by the peoples who had settled there hundreds of years earlier. About 40 city-states (cities that function as separate kingdoms) had developed in the valley. Some of the strongest belonged to the Culhua, Acolhua, Chalca, and Tepanecs. The Tepanecs had built a small empire in the region.

The Aztecs were forced to settle on very poor land in a place called Chapultepec (which means grasshopper hill). The Culhua claimed this land, but they had little use for the rocky soil. However, they still had rights to the land, and the Aztecs were squatters—people who settle on someone else's land without permission. Because of the rocky soil, raising crops in Chapultepec was hard. The Aztecs, though, considered the challenge part of their destiny. They settled in and Chapultepec became their home for 40 years.

The Aztecs' time at Chapultepec ended when an evil sorcerer, or wizard, named Copil arrived in the land. Copil believed that the Aztecs were responsible for the death of his mother and wanted revenge on them. According to the legend, he used evil magic to create trouble between the Aztecs and the local chiefs. Copil arranged for troops of warriors to attack the Aztecs, believing that the entire culture would be wiped out.

However, Copil's powers as a wizard were not strong enough to overcome the sun god, Huitzilopochtli. The sun god revealed the evil plot to his priests, who, in turn, warned the Aztec warriors about the coming attack.

Searching for Aztlan

According to a map drawn by Alexander von Humboldt (1769–1859), an influential German geographer, Aztlan was located near the Great Salt Lake in Utah. He based this on the writings of a 17th-century Spanish priest. At least one modern scholar has suggested that Aztlan was located closer to the north of the Valley of Mexico. Another says information about the true location of Aztlan may have been lost forever in 1428, when the Aztec ruler Itzcoatl (ca. 1360–ca. 1440) supposedly destroyed many of his people's historical documents. But most historians say that Aztlan was not a real place. It was just a name for the mythical first home of the Aztecs.

Huitzilopochtli ordered his priests to have Copil killed. Warriors found the wizard and cut off his head. They also cut out his heart. The chief priest took Copil's heart to Lake Texcoco and threw it as far as he could.

Meanwhile, the Culhua attacked and killed the Aztec leader. Homeless again, the Aztecs pleaded with their enemies to give them some land on which to live. The Aztecs were forced to settle on land that was even worse than Chapultepec. Their new home, Tizaapan, was covered with volcanic rocks and crawling with poisonous snakes.

Despite the harsh conditions at Tizaapan, the Aztecs stayed for nearly 25 years. They cleared the land for farming and killed off the snakes. The Culhua king believed that the Aztecs would see this harsh land and move on, and was surprised when he learned that they were still in Tizaapan. He asked the Aztecs to join in an alliance with him, which the Aztecs agreed to do. Together, they would have the most fearsome army in the Valley of Mexico.

By now, the Aztecs had adopted many aspects of the cultures of the Toltecs in Tula and the Olmecs in Teotihuacan. They added Quetzalcoatl, the Toltecs' favorite god, to their long list of gods. These gods advised and led their followers. They also demanded blood sacrifices, which created new problems between the Aztecs and the Culhua.

IN THEIR OWN WORDS

The Travels of the Aztecs

An ancient Aztec song describes the wanderings of the Aztecs before they reached the Valley of Mexico. Here is a part of it:

As they came,
as they went along their road,
they were no longer received
   everywhere,
they were rejected everywhere,
no one knew their face.
Everywhere they were asked:
"Who are you?

From where do you come?"
Thus nowhere could they settle,
they were always thrown out,
everywhere they were persecuted.

The song goes on to list some of the places the Aztecs passed through, including Tula and Chapultepec.

(Source: Carrasco, David, and Eduardo Matos Moctezuma. *Moctezuma's Mexico: Visions of the Aztecs World.* Rev. ed. Boulder, Colo.: University of Colorado Press, 2003.)

This statue of the god Quetzalcoatl was made by the Toltecs. The Aztecs adopted many of the Toltec gods.

Following orders from the god Huitzilopochtli, the Aztec priests asked the king of the Culhua if he would marry his daughter to their sun god. The king thought his daughter was receiving a great honor. The marriage would cement the link between the two tribes forever.

The young Culhua bride arrived in Tizaapan for the wedding, but it was not the ceremony her father expected. The king of Culhua arrived with wedding gifts, including tobacco, flowers, paper, rubber, and food. He was given a chance to worship his daughter and her

CONNECTIONS

The Eagle Image

In some versions of the story that describes the Aztecs' arrival at their new home, the eagle held a snake in its beak. Today, the symbol of the nation of Mexico shows this version of the story. The emblem, which appears on the country's flag and coins, shows an eagle sitting on a cactus, holding a snake in its beak.

groom, Huitzilopochtli, in a shrine (a holy building dedicated to a god). In the shrine, he saw a young priest wrapped in his own daughter's skin. The Aztecs had sacrificed the Culhua king's daughter.

The fury of the king over his daughter's death was so great that he ordered his Culhua warriors to attack the Aztecs and show no mercy. The warriors were told to hunt down the Aztecs and kill them all. The Aztecs fled and hid in the swampland of Lake Texcoco for weeks. Again, the Aztecs were homeless.

THE CACTUS, THE EAGLE, AND A HOMELAND

The Aztecs were now in the lands of the Tepanecs. Their ruler let them live on an island in the middle of Lake Texcoco, a swampy marsh. In return, they were required to pay tribute and help the Tepanecs fight their enemies.

As they huddled in the marsh, the Aztecs finally received the sign for which they had been waiting. One of their priests had a vision of Huitzilopochtli. The god told the priest to have the Aztecs look for an eagle that lived in a prickly pear cactus and fed on brightly colored birds, scattering their feathers. On one of the marsh islands, the Aztecs saw an eagle perched on a cactus. The cactus grew on the exact spot where the heart of the sorcerer Copil had landed after the Aztecs killed him. In the eagle's claws was a bird with bright feathers.

Diego Durán (ca. 1537–1588), a Spanish priest, later recorded the Aztecs' story of what they felt when they saw the priest's vision fulfilled: "How did we merit so much good fortune? Who made us worthy of such grace and goodness and excellence? . . . We have found our city and site. . ." (quoted in *The History of the Indies of New Spain*).

To the Aztecs, the eagle represented the sun and their sun god, Huitzilopochtli. The cactus stood for the hearts that they would

offer to the god. And the bird in the eagle's claws represented the fallen enemy warriors who would provide the hearts. The location was special, too. The reeds of the swamp reminded them of the city of Tula, the old Toltec city the Aztecs had reached during their travels. Tula's name meant "place of rushes." Near the cactus, the Aztecs built a temple to Huitzilopochtli. On this site, they would later build the Templo Mayor, or Great Temple, in honor of their sun god.

The Aztecs gained several new names once they ended their travels and settled in central Mexico. The people who lived in the capital of Tenochtitlan were called the Tenochca. They took their name from the city, which means "place of the prickly pear cactus." The Tenochca, together with the people of the neighboring city of Tlatelolco, formed the people known today as Aztecs.

The term *Aztec* comes from *Aztlan,* the place where the Aztecs first lived. But the Aztecs did not generally call themselves Aztecs. The word

The national flag of Mexico features an eagle-and-snake design that recalls the mythical founding of Mexico City by the Aztecs.

CONNECTIONS

Mexica and Mexico

Mexico was sometimes used as a name for the Mexica city of Tenochtitlan. That word is the source of the name of the modern nation of Mexico. Today, descendants of the Aztecs are still sometimes called *Mexica*.

was first commonly used in the 19th century, and referred to the Mexica and similar Nahuatl-speaking groups around them in central Mexico.

Aztec was also the name given to the entire empire of the Mexica people—what is referred to in this book as the Aztec Empire. In this book, the Mexica people and their empire will be referred to by the name they are known today—the Aztecs.

PART · 1

HISTORY

BUILDING AN AZTEC HOMELAND

THE TRIPLE ALLIANCE

THE SPANISH CONQUEST

CHAPTER 1

BUILDING AN AZTEC HOMELAND

ARCHAEOLOGISTS HAVE LONG BEEN FASCINATED WITH THE ancient cultures of Mesoamerica. These scientists study the remains of art, buildings, and items used by ancient people in their daily lives. Archaeologists believe that the earliest people in present-day Mexico arrived in about 21,000 B.C.E. They base this belief on bones found at Tlapacoya, southeast of modern Mexico City.

For about 14,000 years, the early people of today's Mexico were nomads—they moved from place to place searching for the best food sources. These nomads were hunter-gatherers. Much of the game they hunted is still common in the area, including deer, rabbits, rats, ducks, geese, and gophers. They took turtles, mussels, and fish from the water. They also hunted three animal species that are now extinct: an antelope species, a variety of horse, and massive mammoths.

Eventually, the people learned how to domesticate certain plants—taking seeds from wild crops, planting them, and taking care of the plants that grew. Farming requires people to stay in one place while the plants grow, so between 7000 and 5000 B.C.E., some people who farmed began living in small, temporary villages until the harvest. They grew chilies, squash, and avocados. They also domesticated two grains—amaranth and *teocintle*. Once domesticated, the grains became their staple foods. *Teocintle* slowly evolved into the grain now called corn.

Over time, the seasonal farming villages became more permanent. People experimented with growing more vegetables, including beans, pumpkins, and gourds. They began raising fruits, such as the *zapotl*, a sweet, plum-like fruit. They also grew sunflowers, which were valued for their seeds.

OPPOSITE
The Pyramid of the Sun rises above the site of the ancient city of Teotihuacan, in today's Mexico.

CONNECTIONS

Honoring Corn

From its origins in Mexico, corn has become one of the most widely grown crops in the world. In many countries, it is called *maize*. This comes from the Spanish word *matz*, which came from the Taíno Indian word *mahiz*.

Before the Spanish arrived, corn had already spread far beyond its origins in Mexico. It was grown by native peoples across the Americas.

The Aztecs valued corn so much that they referred to corn dough as "our flesh." They also worshipped the goddess Xilonen, who watched over the corn harvest. Some Mexican-Americans in California still honor Xilonen by holding a ceremony for teenage girls who are named for her. The event marks the girl's passage from childhood to adulthood.

People also developed tools to use in their homes. One of the most ancient tools was a grinding slab called *metlatl* in Nahuatl. The people also began weaving baskets and mats and doing woodwork. They made traps, fishing rods, spears, and darts. They tanned the hides from the animals they hunted and crafted the hides into sandals, belts, and slings for hunting.

As farming replaced hunting and gathering as the main way to get food, people began domesticating farm animals. Early Mesoamericans raised dogs and turkeys for food. They did not have large animals they could ride or use to pull carts, such as horses, oxen, or cattle. So they traveled along rivers and lakes on rafts and canoes, or walked.

The skills, culture, and beliefs of the Aztecs were shaped by the great Mesoamerican cultures that came before them—particularly the Olmecs, Toltecs, and Mixtecs. To understand the Aztecs, it is first necessary to know something about their ancestors.

THE OLMECS

Starting about 1500 B.C.E., the Olmecs developed the first complex society in Mesoamerica. Historians do not know what the Olmecs called themselves. The name used for them today comes from the Aztec word *Olmeca*, which means "rubber people"—the Olmecs lived in the region where rubber trees grew.

The Olmecs created an advanced culture based on farming, particularly corn. The upper classes of rulers, warriors, and priests (sometimes called shamans) lived in cities, while the common farmers lived in rural areas. Remains of the Olmec culture—earth mounds and pyramids—have been found at several sites, including two known today as San Lorenzo and La Venta.

The Olmecs were builders. La Venta, located on an island in a swamp, featured a cone-shaped mound of clay more than 100 feet high. Historians have found several earthworks, or mounds, in San Lorenzo that served a religious purpose. The most important mound there reaches 150 feet high. It was built by hundreds of workers using hand tools and carrying the dirt up the slope by the basketful. San Lorenzo also had a stone system for draining wastewater. This drainage system is the oldest ever found in the Americas.

Giant stone heads like this one are the most well-known artifacts of the Olmec culture. Archaeologists think the giant heads represented the Olmec kings.

The Olmecs were also sculptors. They carved massive stone heads, some measuring as much a 10 feet high. The heads have flat faces, broad noses, and thick lips. The heads appear to be wearing helmets, and several archaeologists think the heads represent Olmec kings. The stone heads found in San Lorenzo are especially remarkable because they were made from stone originally found about 50 miles away. Workers had to cut the stone from the mountains and haul it to its final site. Archaeologists believe the Olmecs did this by putting log rollers under the stone as they pulled it along.

There are no definite dates for the Olmec culture. They probably thrived from about 1500 to 400 B.C.E., but their impact on other emerging cultures in the region lasted long after the Olmecs had disappeared. They introduced the idea of human sacrifice—killing humans as a gift to their gods. They practiced bloodletting, which

CONNECTIONS

The *Metlatl*

The *metlatl* is one of the oldest household tools in the Americas. It has been used since about 7000 B.C.E. In some places, it is still used today.

In ancient times, the women first soaked corn kernels overnight in a clay pot filled with water and the chemical lime or ashes from a fire. The lime or ashes helped soften the kernels and also added calcium. In the morning, the women put the softened ker-

nels into the *metlatl* and used a rock shaped like a rolling pin with flattened sides (the *metlapilli*—a Nahuatl word that means "child of the metlatl") to crush them.

The *metlatl* usually had three legs to hold the stone at an angle so that crushing the grain was easier. The women took the prepared corn and used it to make tortillas or tamales—dishes that are still eaten today.

means making a person bleed as part of a religious ceremony. Both the Maya and the Aztecs also practiced sacrifices and bloodletting. The Olmecs also began the idea of building temples in the shape of pyramids. From the top of these tall buildings, they offered sacrifices and hoped to get closer to their gods. They also created a system for writing down ideas in stone using images—an early form of writing.

THE BUSY CITY OF TEOTIHUACAN

As the Olmec culture disappeared, large city centers arose in the Mesoamerican region. These central, independent cities dominated surrounding towns and villages, in an arrangement sometimes called city-states. The greatest city-states from 300 B.C.E. to 250 C.E. were Teotihuacan, Tikal, Monte Albán, and Cuicuilco. Wealthy classes emerged, gaining their riches primarily through land ownership (running big farms) or military means (winning wars). But these city-states grew and thrived far more through trade than by conquering others.

In the Valley of Mexico, the two major city-states were Teotihuacan and Cuicuilco. At more than eight square miles in area, Teotihuacan was the largest city built in the Americas before the arrival of Christopher Columbus (1451–1506) in 1492. It was located in a fertile valley close to sources of water, making it easy to farm. The local area also had large quantities of green obsidian, and this volcanic glass was traded for food, highly prized tropical bird feathers, and seashells. Teotihuacan became known for its outstanding artisans (skilled workers who make things by hand), particularly those who worked with obsidian. The city was located on a main route to the coast. Travelers and traders moving between the Valley of Mexico and the Pacific coast went right through Teotihuacan, helping trade expand.

Cuicuilco emerged a little before Teotihuacan and may have had as many as 20,000 residents. It had a number of pyramids and a canal that carried water to irrigate farms. The city's location, however, led to its end. Sometime between 100 and 50 B.C.E., the local volcano erupted and destroyed Cuicuilco. Lava covered most of the farmland, making it impossible to grow food locally. The people who survived the eruption moved to Teotihuacan.

By 1 C.E., Teotihuacan had more than 40,000 residents. Five hundred years later, the city's population may have reached 200,000, making it one of the largest cities in the world. Teotihuacan continued to grow in an organized fashion. It featured broad avenues and large pyramids that were temples to the gods. At the pyramids, people made offerings (left gifts) for their gods. Human sacrifices may have been made at the pyramids as well. Another large structure, the Palace of the Jaguars, was at the far end of the Avenida de los Muertos—the Avenue of the Dead. Priests paraded along the avenue during religious rituals.

Teotihuacan thrived until about 650 C.E., when enemies from the north attacked and a great fire destroyed the city. For some unknown reason, the people did not rebuild the city. Instead, the population began moving to other growing cities. Within a few hundred years, the great city of Teotihuacan was deserted.

New Old Writing

In 2006, archaeologists found a large slab covered with carvings that were believed to be the work of the Olmecs. The stone's carvings date to about 600 B.C.E. and feature images or symbols sometimes called glyphs. The stone slab has been named the Cascajal block, after the spot in Mexico where it was found.

The slab weighs 26 pounds and is 14 inches long, 8 inches wide, and 5 inches thick. Some archaeologists call the carvings an early form of writing, though the Olmecs did not have the type of alphabet used today. So far, the glyphs have not been decoded. Scientists hope that additional finds will give them clues about the meaning of the ancient writing.

The stunning remains of the Pyramids of the Sun and Moon in the ancient city of Teotihuancan are now a protected World Heritage Site.

Some historians believe the people of Teotihuacan may have contributed to their city's ruin. In their quest to build the most beautiful city, they damaged the area's environment. They dug up the land surrounding the city to get the lime that was needed for making plaster—a major ingredient in the city's buildings. As the city grew, the need for plaster increased and more land was destroyed. Eventually, the damage was too great. The soil on the surrounding land could not grow enough food, and hunters could not find enough game to feed the people. It became harder to bring food to the city, so people began leaving.

THE TOLTECS

By 900, a new culture was emerging in northern Mexico, in the city of Tula. The people there were the Toltecs. They spread their culture through wars and trade, and influenced many other cultures in what is today Mexico and Guatemala. The Toltecs took certain aspects of the Teotihuacan culture, such as styles of art and architecture, and added them to their own culture.

The Toltecs also spread their belief in the god Quetzalcoatl. The god's name means "quetzal-feathered serpent" (the quetzal is a colorful bird found in Central America). The Toltecs believed this god was a skilled warrior and created human beings. According to Aztec mythology, Quetzalcoatl was the son of the leader of an ancient people; he left home so that he could become the ruler of the Toltecs. Under his rule, the people were respected as great artists and scientists. Quetzalcoatl was later fooled by Tezcatlipoca, a god of evil and trickery, who took the form of a sly human. Tezcatlipoca tricked Quetzalcoatl into leaving the Toltec lands, but Quetzalcoatl promised to return at a later date.

The city of Tula grew as a center for crafts and religious events. By 1000, the population reached about 60,000 people. Artisans shaped obsidian into knives and spearheads, as well as bowls, plates, jugs, and storage jars. These goods were traded in the city's marketplace.

The Pyramids of Teotihuacan

The Aztecs gave the city of Teotihuacan its name; it means "the place where the gods were created." They believed the city was located in an ancient area where two older gods sacrificed themselves to become new gods, the sun and the moon. The Aztecs used the names of those powerful gods to describe Teotihuacan's two largest pyramids, the Pyramid of the Sun and the Pyramid of the Moon.

The builders of the pyramids wanted to show their respect for the gods, so they painted the temples bright red, making them glow in the sun. The people of Teotihuacan built the Pyramid of the Sun above a cave that was thought to be a link to the underworld, the place where spirits lived.

The pyramids of Teotihuacan and other ancient remains there led the United Nations Educational, Scientific, and Cultural Organization (UNESCO) to name the city a World Heritage Site. This means Teotihuacan is recognized as having special historical and cultural importance.

What Is Your Name?

Toltec was not the culture's own name for itself. As with many ancient peoples, what they called themselves is unknown. The name used for them today came from the Aztecs. In Nahuatl, *toltecatl* is the word for "craftsman" or "artisan." *Toltec* was the name the Aztecs later used for the people who passed on the Teotihuacan tradition of quality craftsmanship.

People from the outlying farms and villages flocked to Tula for the many religious festivals held there. Priests paraded through the center of the city's main plaza and onto the two pyramids where human sacrifices were held. Each temple featured *chacmools*. A *chacmool* was a stone figure with a bowl where its stomach would be. During a human sacrifice, the victim's heart was flung into the bowl of the *chacmool*. Temples also had racks for displaying the skulls of sacrifice victims. These rituals eventually became part of the Aztecs' religious beliefs.

Tula had two ball courts where teams competed by passing a rubber ball through a hoop. This game was mainly religious, not sporting. It celebrated the victories of god-heroes over the gods of death. Teams fought hard to win because the losing team was usually sacrificed at the temple.

The empire of the Toltecs came to an end some time between 1150 and 1200. Enemies overran Tula. The city was burned and was never rebuilt. The Toltec culture faded away, but many of its customs were carried on by other peoples.

The Endangered Quetzal

The quetzal, a sacred bird to the ancient peoples of Mesoamerica, is one of the most beautiful birds in the Americas. Its feathers were so valued by the Aztecs that only priests and emperors could wear them. Instead of killing the birds to acquire the feathers, people plucked them from the bird's tail. In the days of the Aztecs, killing a quetzal was a crime punishable by death.

The quetzal lives in remote rain forests from southern Mexico to Bolivia. Its tail feathers are extremely long, shimmering emerald-green plumes. When the bird flies, the tail shows white underneath.

Modern humans have not honored the quetzal the way the Aztecs did. The colorful feathers have been used in the fashion trade and fetch very high prices. The value of quetzal feathers has encouraged poaching (illegally capturing animals). These poachers often kill the birds to take their feathers. The combination of poaching and loss of habitat has put this Aztec treasure on the endangered species list.

This chest plate (or *chimalli*) was made by Mixtec craftspeople using gold and turquoise. The Mixtecs were well-known for their ability to make beautiful gold objects.

THE MIXTECS

The Mixtecs lived in three mountainous areas of present-day Oaxaca. The region is sometimes called the Mixteca. Their culture was at its height between 940 and 1500. The Mixtecs first lived on hilltops before spreading out into nearby valleys. They never developed large cities to rival Tula or Teotihuacan, but they had many other accomplishments. For example, they were known for remarkable gold work.

The Mixtecs also developed a writing system that influenced other Mesoamerican cultures. They used a combination of written signs and pictures to record historical information. Records of the marriages, births, and deaths of nobles were painted on deerskin. Wars, victories, and changes from one king to the next were also recorded. Every document was dated with the day and year, which has enabled historians to follow the events that affected the Mixtec people. Only eight of the original Mixtec historic documents survive to this day.

Records of the Past

The Mixtecs and other people of Mesoamerica recorded information in what is today called a *codex* (the plural is *codices*). A codex is an ancient manuscript text in book form. The Mixtec codices were made from strips of bark, paper, cloth, or deerskin that are about 13 feet long and about 6 inches high. These were folded in accordion-style pleats, so that when opened, the reader saw two pages at a time. The two outer pages were glued to pieces of wood that served as covers.

The Aztecs and other people of central Mexico also produced codices, even after the Spanish arrived. These looked more like modern books than the older accordion-style codices.

Today, codices from before and after the Spanish conquest provide historians with information on life in Mexico hundreds of years ago. Some of these codices were taken to Europe and placed in book collections, where they were forgotten for several centuries. Today, a codex is sometimes named for the city where it is kept, such as the Paris Codex and the Dresden Codex.

The Mixtecs were one of the peoples the Aztecs conquered. While many Mixtecs no doubt were sacrificed at Aztec temples, some Mixtec goldsmiths went to the Aztec capital, Tenochtitlan, to make jewelry for their new rulers. Mixtec nobles who remained in their mountain regions paid their tribute to Aztec rulers in gold. That wealth was just part of the riches the Aztecs acquired as they built their empire.

BUILDING TENOCHTITLAN

One mountain range, the Sierra Madre Occidental, runs along the Pacific Ocean to the west. The other, the Sierra Madre Oriental, rises in the east. Another range, the Sierra Ajusco, marks the southern edge of the Aztec's territory. The region is now called the Valley of Mexico. Actually, it is a basin—a large area of land marked by sloping sides.

The Valley of Mexico had five lakes, and the Aztecs chose to settle on two islands in swampy Lake Texcoco. These island locations had good conditions for raising crops. They also had some problems. The swamp was full of insects and building materials were hard to find. But the Aztecs had canoes and could travel easily through the swamp. And an island was easier to defend than a site on land.

The Aztecs founded their new city, Tenochtitlan, in 1325. The city measured five square miles. Its name came from *tenochtli*, the Nahuatl word for "prickly pear cactus." As it grew, Tenochtitlan looked like a mountain erupting from the lake, and it dominated the landscape. It became the capital of the Aztec Empire.

A sister city, called Tlatelolco, was started on a neighboring island. It later became the Aztec center for trade and grew to be nearly the same size as Tenochtitlan.

Water was critical for the Aztecs' survival. Canals linked together smaller plots of land called *chinampas*. These were small islands the Aztecs built in shallow waters so they could grow crops. Small footbridges connected the *chinampas* so farmers could easily move between them as they worked. The waterways between the *chinampas* provided transportation routes for the island's inhabitants. Fish and waterfowl were plentiful on the lake. These added protein to the Aztecs' mainly vegetarian diet.

Stone water channels brought fresh water into the city for drinking and bathing. The Aztecs bathed every day, and wealthy Aztecs frequently had steambaths in their homes. Sewage and trash were placed on barges, and much of the sewage became fertilizer for the crops raised on the *chinampas*.

Aztec engineers produced an island city much like Venice, Italy, which is famous for its canals. In Tenochtitlan, canals were used as streets and people traveled everywhere by canoe. Architects created three causeways (raised roads) to connect the city to the mainland. The transportation links enabled the Aztecs to carry food and goods to and from the city's market, trade with other peoples, and go to war.

Tenochtitlan was one of the finest cities of ancient Mexico. The central part of the city featured massive stone temples, sprawling palaces for the emperor and the royal family, gardens,

Mixtecs in the News

A Mixtec site being studied by archaeologists today shows that the Mixtecs used cremation, or burning a corpse, in their burial rituals. The burial site currently being excavated (dug out and examined) shows that cremation was used as far back as 3,000 years ago.

According to Andrew Balkansky, an archaeologist from Southern Illinois University, it is possible the Mixtecs believed that burning a corpse released the person's soul from the body. "The idea was that, basically, you'd have someone's soul ascend to the heavens in the smoke," said Balkansky (quoted in *National Geographic News,* April 9, 2008). Historians think the Mixtecs believed cremation brought their spirits closer to the gods.

CONNECTIONS

Open Markets

In the 14th century, the open market in Tenochtitlan attracted 25,000 people, who gathered to buy and sell goods. Everything the Aztecs produced could be traded in the market. Artisans set up stalls and traded lengths of fine cloth or sacks of dried maize. Vendors sold seashells and silver, bright blue turquoise, and vegetables grown on nearby farms.

The market was a bustling place where slaves, commoners, and royalty mixed in an effort to get a good deal. Haggling, or arguing over an item's price, was essential. No deal was considered final without this kind of discussion.

Today, almost every Mexican city and town has an open market. Farmers bring fruits and vegetables to sell. Clothing, jewelry, leather goods, and pottery are also for sale. Just as in Aztec times, buyers and sellers expect to discuss how much an item is worth. Prices go up and down with the discussion, until an agreement is reached.

Which Is the Older Sister?

By traditional accounts, Tlatelolco was founded in 1358, more than 30 years after Tenochtitlan. In recent years, however, archaeologists have uncovered evidence that challenges this date. In 1992, they found remains of a pyramid at Tlatelolco that dated from 1325. And in 2007, the remains of an even older pyramid were found there, suggesting it was built before Tenochtitlan was established.

and even a zoo. The outer edges of the island had dozens of small farms and small homes made of adobe, a building material made by mixing sand, straw, and water and letting it bake in the sun.

The Aztec gods and goddesses were always present, and the city had many temples, plazas, and sacred ball courts. For the Aztecs, Tenochtitlan became a holy city and was the place where all major religious festivals were held. Since schools were most often attached to temples, the city also developed into a center of learning.

The first temple was built in 1325 and was dedicated to Huitzilopochtli—the god who had guided the Aztecs to their new home. That earliest temple was not a grand pyramid made of stone, but a simple altar (a platform where religious ceremonies are held) and a hut made from sticks and mud. Over time, the Aztecs built newer and larger temples right over the old ones. Before the beginning of the 15th century, the Aztecs had already built a temple that rose 50 feet high. Later, an even larger temple reached into the skies. To the Aztecs, the heavens above were sacred, and the temple's great height brought them closer to that holy place.

Over time, the population of Tenochtitlan expanded. At the height of the Aztec Empire, nearly 200,000 people lived on the crowded island. The city was divided into quarters. Each of the four quarters was further divided into neighborhoods, called *calpulli*. Each quarter had 12 to 15 *calpulli*. A *calpulli* had a temple and priests, a school, homes, gardens, and streets. Although major religious events were held at the temple in the city's center, smaller festivals were celebrated within the *calpulli*.

Like other empire builders, the Aztecs believed their gods had chosen them for success. Keeping the gods' favor was important to the ruling classes, so they would continue to enjoy the benefits of ruling other peoples. At times, that meant conquering enemies and offering some of them as sacrifices. Many Mesoamerican peoples believed that the gods thrived on human blood. Without blood, the gods would be dissatisfied and the people would suffer.

But the Aztecs also had practical reasons for seeking to expand their empire. As they conquered lands, they received valuable tribute that made their rulers rich. The rulers enjoyed the power their wealth and control gave them. They also enjoyed the idea that they were blessed by the gods.

THE FIRST *TLATOANI*

About 50 years after the founding of Tenochtitlan, the Aztec named their first *tlatoani*, or king. The word *tlatoani* means "he who speaks well." Many historians consider Acamapichtli (r. ca. 1375–1395) to be the first true *tlatoani* of Tenochtitlan. He founded the dynasty, or ruling family, that would eventually build the powerful Aztec Empire. Acamapichtli, though, was not a native of Tenochtitlan or even an Aztec. He was a Culhua.

The Aztecs had a reason for going outside their own tribe to choose a king. To start a noble dynasty they needed a real, legitimate nobleman. They admired the Toltec culture, and Acamapichtli may have been directly related to Toltec leaders.

One of Acamapichtli's strategies to unite the Aztecs was marrying the daughters of 20 *calpulli* leaders. Having many wives was the privilege of royalty. Through marriage, Acamapichtli made sure he had the support of the local leaders. He also made sure that his sons would lead the people, since they would have family ties to all the local leaders.

When Acamapichtli began his rule, the Aztecs were still paying tribute to the more powerful Tepanecs. In exchange, Tenochtitlan enjoyed the protection of the Tepanecs and Aztec merchants could trade in the Tepanec marketplace in Azcapotzalco.

How Is It Pronounced?

Acamapichtli
ah-cah-mah-PEECH-tlee

Cuicuilco
kwee-KWEEL-coh

Huitzilihuitl
wheet-see-LEE-wheetl

Metlatl
MAY-tlahtl

Oaxaca
wah-HAH-kuh

Tenochtitlan
teh-nohch-TEE-tlahn

Tezcatlipoca
tess-kah-tlee-POH-kuh

Tlatelolco
tlah-tay-LOL-ko

Tlatoani
tlah-toh-AH-nee

The Aztecs also sent soldiers to fight in the army of the Tepanecs. This arrangement helped the Aztec warriors gain experience in military matters. Eventually, Acamapichtli decided to use those skilled warriors for his own benefit. With an experienced army behind him, Acamapichtli went to war against the nearby Chalca people. The war began right after Acamapichtli took power and went on past his death. It was finally won by the Aztecs under Huitzilihuitl (r. 1395–1417), Acamapichtli's son.

Acamapichtli proved to be an excellent choice as leader. He introduced many changes that benefited the people of Tenochtitlan. He developed a basic legal code, and later *tlatoani* would add new laws to the code. Under Acamapichtli, the importance of religious rites, including human sacrifice, grew. With the need to thank the gods for the Aztecs' good fortune, Acamapichtli thought all citizens should take part in religious ceremonies.

IN THEIR OWN WORDS

Hymns to Huitzilopochtli

Huitzilopochtli, the god who led the Aztecs out of Aztlan, was the god of war and the sun. This excerpt from a longer hymn suggests his role as the sun god. (Plumes are long feathers.)

> Huitzilopochtli, the young warrior,
> Who acts above! He follows his path!
> "Not in vain did I dress myself in yellow
>   plumes,
> for I am he who has caused the sun to rise."

Other hymns focused on Huitzilopochtli's role as the god of war. Here is part of one of them.

> A maker of war,
> An arranger of battles,

> A lord of battles;
> And of him it was said
> That he hurled his flaming serpent,
> His fire stick;
> Which means war,
> Blood and burning;
> And when his festival was
>   celebrated,
> Captives were slain. . . .

(Source: Garibay K., Angel Maria, editor. *Veinte himnos sacros de los Nahuas*. Mexico City: National University of Mexico Press, 1958; and "The Hymn of Huitzilopochtli." *Rig Veda Americanus*. Daniel G. Brinton, translator. Available online. URL: http://www.sacred-texts.com/nam/Aztecs/rva/rva01.htm. Accessed October 14, 2008.)

In the city, Acamapichtli started many building projects. The population was growing, and the city needed more land. Acamapichtli ordered that the island's size be increased by filling in swampland with soil. He also ordered city houses made of cane and reeds to be replaced by stronger houses made of stone. This way, if there were severe storms, the homes would protect the island's people. At the same time, the Aztecs began building larger stone temples on the site of the first pyramids.

Acamapichtli gave his dynasty a solid foundation. A council of elders—a group of wise and respected men in the community—chose each new Aztec *tlatoani* based on his battle skills and leadership ability. When Acamapichtli died in 1395, he left behind many sons who formed the basis of the royal family. One of those sons, Huitzilihuitl, was chosen by the council of elders to follow his father as *tlatoani*.

Legendary Leader

According to Aztec legend, a priest named Tenoch was the first leader of the Aztecs who settled in Tenochtitlan. But he was not considered a *tlatoani*. For a time, Tenochtitlan and Tlatelolco had separate governments (although by about the 1470s they were united) and Tenoch ruled only Tenochtitlan.

Tenoch was said to be a highly regarded chief who was elected to power by the council of elders—a group of wise and respected men in the community. In Aztec art, he is shown wearing white robes and seated on a reed mat—two symbols of his leadership.

Tenoch is traditionally believed to have died in about 1370. But historians disagree about whether he is a real person or a mythical leader.

CHAPTER 2

THE TRIPLE ALLIANCE

WHEN HUITZILIHUITL BECAME *TLATOANI*, THE AZTECS were still subjects of the Tepanecs in Azcapotzalco and paid tribute to them. In a clever diplomatic move, Huitzilihuitl married the daughter of the Tepanec ruler Tezozomoc (r. ca. 1367–1426). He hoped that the marriage would make Tezozomoc reduce the high taxes the Aztecs paid.

The idea worked. Tezozomoc married off his daughters to nobility in both Tlatelolco and Tenochtitlan—the two cities in which the Aztecs lived. Looking with favor on his children, the Tepanec ruler reduced the amount of tribute the Aztecs had to pay. However, Huitzilihuitl still had to send warriors to fight in the Tepanec army. These Aztec warriors helped Tezozomoc conquer the neighboring tribes and collect tribute from his neighbors.

Huitzilihuitl had impressed the council of elders with his talents as a warrior. And he introduced a major change that advanced Aztec warfare. During his reign, the military began to use 30-foot-long canoes that carried up to a dozen men. This change gave the Aztecs a huge advantage. Wars were always fought on fields that could be reached by walking. An army that walked completely around a large lake needed rest before getting on with the business of fighting. The Aztec military began transporting its men in canoes, and the soldiers arrived ready for battle.

When Huitzilihuitl died in 1417, the Aztec elders elected Chimalpopoca (r. 1417–1426) as *tlatoani*. Chimalpopoca was chosen because he was Tezozomoc's favorite grandson. Since Chimalpopoca was not yet an adult, the Aztecs needed an older man to serve as the regent—a

OPPOSITE
Motecuhzoma II, shown here in a Spanish painting from the 16th century, was a gifted leader, a great builder, and a skilled warrior.

How Is It Pronounced?

Axayacatl
   ah-shah-YAH-cahtl
Chimalpopoca
   chee-mahl-poh-POH-
   kuh
Itzcoatl
   eetz-KOH-ahtl
Motecuhzoma
   moh-tehk-SOH-muh
Nezahualcoyotl
   neh-sah-hual-KOH-
   yohtl
Tezozomoc
   tay-soh-SOH-mohk
Tlacaelel
   tlah-cah-El-el
Tlacopan
   tlah-KOH-pahn

person appointed to rule until the real ruler is ready. Tezozomoc appointed himself regent.

Tezozomoc was an oppressive ruler. He placed great demands—mostly heavy taxes—on his people. By the time Chimalpopoca was mature enough to rule, he was considered too incompetent to assume the responsibilities, and so he never became *tlatoani*. As a result, Tezozomoc ruled for almost 60 years. No one knows how old he was when he died—although some historians claim he lived to be over 100 years old. When he finally died, he left two problems behind for the Tepanecs. First, he never trained anyone to take his place. This lack of planning on his part lead to the second problem. Tezozomoc's son Maxtla (d. 1428) expected to be the next ruler, but the Tepanec council of elders chose one of his brothers instead. Maxtla took care of the situation by killing his brother and any other Tepanec enemies and taking over as leader.

By this time, Chimalpopoca had become an adult. He had supported the choice of Maxtla's brother, and Maxtla considered the Aztec *tlatoani* to be his enemy. Shortly after Maxtla killed his brother, someone sneaked into the Aztec royal palace and killed both Chimalpopoca and his infant son. All eyes turned toward Maxtla as the murderer, but the Aztecs were too weak to take on the Tepanec army. In addition, Maxtla used his army to cut off the Aztecs from their usual sources of trade. The Aztecs were filled with a desire for revenge, but would have to wait.

FORMING THE TRIPLE ALLIANCE

The Aztec council of elders elected Itzcoatl (r. 1427–1440) to be the next *tlatoani*. Itzcoatl was the son of Acamapichtli and a slave woman. Itzcoatl worshipped the god Huitzilopochtli and wanted that god to receive the highest honors offered by the Aztec people. He also wanted to throw off the rule of Maxtla and the Tepanecs. His nephew Tlacaelel (ca. 1397–1487) helped him carry out his plans.

Itzcoatl soon gained two allies in his struggle against Maxtla and the Tepanecs. One was the Texcoco prince Nezahualcoyotl (1402–1472). When he was a young man, Nezahualcoyotl's father was killed by the Tepanecs and he was forced to live in exile (away from his homeland) for many years. After Itzcoatl became *tlatoani* in Tenochtitlan, Nezahualcoyotl regained his place as ruler of Texcoco. Nezahualcoyotl hated the Tepanecs, and Itzcoatl was his uncle. It seemed fitting that the two would form an alliance.

The leader of Tlacopan then joined the alliance. In 1428, the three banded together to rid themselves of the Tepanecs. They formed the Triple Alliance, the political unit that led the Aztecs to expand their empire from coast to coast.

For the battle with the Tepanecs, drums called the Aztecs warriors to action. They and their allies met in the fields near Maxtla's troops. The Aztecs screamed with all their might and charged the Tepanec warriors. Maxtla's forces were so stunned by the Aztecs' actions that they failed to react. The Aztec warriors fell on them, killing and wounding many of Maxtla's men.

This was so shocking because it was not typical of warfare at the time. Generally, the warriors in front of an army made a huge amount of noise—drums, stamping feet, chanting, and whistling. While this happened, another group of warriors slipped around to the sides of the battlefield and tried to surround the opposition. Maxtla's troops may have been stunned because the Aztecs normally drew the enemy to them and surrounded them, but this time they attacked head on.

The Tepanecs retreated into the city of Azcapotzalco with the Aztec warriors in hot pursuit. The Aztecs destroyed buildings and tore apart temples in Azcapotzalco. They killed the people and left the bodies to rot on the ground. This also was not typical of the time. The Aztecs rarely killed their opponents, preferring to wound them. The opponents could then be used as slaves, sacrifices, workers, or to fill out the ranks of the Aztec army.

Maxtla hid in one of the palace steambaths, but he was quickly found and brought to Nezahualcoyotl, the ruler of Texcoco. The young prince finally took revenge for his father's death and killed Maxtla. Warriors set fire to the once-great Tepanec city of Azcapotzalco, and it was soon reduced to rubble. Its people lay dead in the streets or became slaves. The city center eventually became a slave market.

The Aztecs and their allies took everything of value that they found in Azcapotzalco. The Triple Alliance divided up the territory once ruled by the Tepanecs and began collecting tribute. Tenochtitlan and Texcoco each took two shares of the Tepanec wealth, and Tlacapan took one share.

New Source of Water

During Chimalpopoca's reign, he began a major building project that greatly helped his people. As Tenochtitlan grew, the demand for fresh water increased. Chimalpopoca built an aqueduct, an artificial channel specifically designed to carry water over long distances. The aqueduct was 7.5 miles long and brought in water from springs located outside the city, near a mountain called Chapultepec. The aqueduct was made from mud, so over the years the rushing water wore away its sides. The Aztecs later built a new aqueduct of stone along the path of the first one.

The Power Behind the *Tlatoani*

Tlacaelel served as a chief advisor for several Aztec *tlatoque* (the plural of *tlatoani*). Some historians consider him to be the true power in the Aztec government during the first decades of the empire.

During Itzcoatl's rule, government officials destroyed all the old documents and records of the Mexica migration. Not all historians agree, though, that this actually happened. If it did, it was most likely Tlacaelel who ordered the destruction of these records. Tlacaelel sought to get rid of any evidence that showed the Aztecs' humble roots as nomads. He wanted the Aztecs—and others—to believe they were always a noble, powerful people.

The change that took place in the Valley of Mexico was dramatic. Instead of everyone paying the Tepanecs and providing soldiers for their army, the three allies enjoyed their first taste of independence. This was not the end of the Tepanec Empire, though. Other Tepanec cities continued to thrive, but they did not have nearly as much power as the Aztecs.

One Tepanec stronghold that resisted the rise of Aztec power was Coyoacan. The Aztecs sent ambassadors to Coyoacan. The city's leaders provided a feast, then insulted their guests. They forced the ambassadors to dress as women and return to Tenochtitlan in that way. Itzcoatl was furious. He immediately declared war.

The Tepanecs in Coyoacan did not fully understand the strength of the enemy they had enraged. The Aztec troops and their allies built large fires around the walls of Coyoacan. They cut off the water to the city and put rotting flesh on the fires. The stink from the burning flesh was unbearable.

Finally, the Tepanec army left the protection of Coyoacan and set out to meet the Aztecs in battle. The Aztecs were smart warriors. A small force circled around and attacked the Tepanecs from behind. With fierce warriors at the front and the rear of their troops, the Tepanec warriors fled for their lives. Once more, the combined forces of the Triple Alliance were too strong for their enemies.

The power of the Triple Alliance spread throughout the Valley of Mexico. Ruling such a large, spread-out group had its problems. The biggest problems were transportation and communication. The limited transportation—either on foot or in a canoe—hindered the ability of *tlatoque* to get from place to place quickly. With little transportation, communicating changes in laws or announcing wars and taxes took time.

The three leaders of the Triple Alliance also wanted their people to follow a standard code of laws. They developed laws that were simple and easy to understand, and each law had a specific punishment. No judge could give harsher sentences to his enemies or easier punishments to his friends. People could not use the law to injure their enemies, since making false accusations against others also brought penalties. Most major crimes were punished by death, either by stoning or strangulation. Most minor crimes had combined penalties of paying the victim for his or her loss and/or becoming a slave. In general, the Aztecs seemed to have obeyed the laws, and their culture did not accept wild or rebellious behavior from adults or children.

In Tenochtitlan, Itzcoatl turned his attention to the needs of his people. He expanded farming by developing more *chinampas* in the southern region of his empire. He also built more roads, temples, and another causeway leading into the capital city. Before Itzcoatl, the Aztecs were subjects ruled by others. Once the Triple Alliance defeated the Tepanecs, the Aztecs became the rulers of their own empire. They emerged as the most powerful of the three allies, and they built a culture that thrived on power and wealth.

A Prince—and a Poet?

Nezahualcoyotl is remembered as one of ancient Mexico's greatest *tlatoque*. He earned fame as an architect, engineer, warrior, and lawmaker in the city-state of Texcoco. During his rule, he established a library, a zoo, and a university for scholars and poets.

He also was once considered a great poet. A 17th-century Aztec-Spanish historian claimed Nezahualcoyotl wrote many works. (That historian was also the *tlatoani*'s great-great-great-great-grandson, Fernando de Alva Ixtlilxochitl, ca. 1568–1648.) For several centuries, people accepted the idea that Nezahualcoyotl was a poet.

In recent years, however, historians have realized that all the poetry said to have been written by him was, in fact, written by others. Nezahualcoyotl may or may not have been a poet. If he was, none of his poems survives. It is likely that Ixtlilxochitl was simply bragging about his famous ancestor.

Nezahualcoyotl, though, is still honored in Mexico. He appears on the 100-peso bill.

A Friend from an Enemy

Tlacopan was actually under Tepanec rule just before the Triple Alliance was formed. But the ruler there was a son of Tezozomoc who thought he had a good claim to the throne of the Tepanecs. Because his claim was ignored by the Tepanec ruler, Maxtla, who was also a son of Tezozomoc, Tlacopan's loyalty to Maxtla was weak. When Aztec forces invaded Tlacopan, they were greeted as allies and not enemies, because the ruler had already agreed to side with Itzcoatl against Maxtla.

MOTECUHZOMA

In 1440, Motecuhzoma Ilhuicamina (r. 1440–1469) became the new *tlatoani*. Motecuhzoma combined noble blood with proven military skill. He was a son of Huitzilihuitl, the second *tlatoani*, and a cousin of Itzcoatl. He was also a member of the council that chose the next *tlatoani*. When the election was discussed, he was the natural choice among the possible candidates.

From the start, Motecuhzoma was determined to expand Aztec rule. Like all empires, the Aztecs believed they had the right to rule over their neighbors. They may even have believed that it was their destiny to rule all the land between the Pacific Ocean and the Gulf of Mexico. Motecuhzoma knew the way to achieve this was by making the gods happy.

As tribute poured into the city of Tenochtitlan, Motecuhzoma put the empire's wealth to work. He began a long-range plan to address the needs of his people. He richly rewarded his soldiers after their conquests and shared some of the empire's wealth with the nobles. He made sure his people were fed, had jobs, and were protected. He built close alliances with the peoples who had been conquered earlier. He strengthened the city with many building projects, including more roads into the city and new housing. He also ordered new temples be built throughout the city.

Motecuhzoma honored the history of the Mexica people. He knew the legends of Aztlan and the story of the seven tribes emerging from the seven caves. He sent an expedition of 60 sorcerers to find Chicomoztoc, the Place of the Seven Caves. There, Motecuhzoma believed, they would find the mother of the god Huitzilopochtli. He gave the sorcerers cloth, gems, and other riches to give to the god's mother.

The expedition backtracked along the path the Mexica had taken. They went to Teotihuacan and Tula—two cities where the Mexica had spent several years as they journeyed south. They continued northward and came to a great lake, where they traveled by canoe to a mountain island. There, they learned that the fortunes of the Aztecs would fall because the god Huitzilopochtli would lose power.

When they returned to Tenochtitlan, the sorcerers told Motecuhzoma of their journey. They reported what they had learned: That the Aztec world was coming to an end. Motecuhzoma was not happy to hear that his people and his favorite god were doomed. Natural disasters that soon struck seemed to lend weight to the sorcerers' words.

Unusual events in nature were long considered a sign of unhappy gods or evil human activities. Soon after the sorcerers' return, a cloud of locusts swept into the valley and ate all the crops. These were most likely cicadas that followed their natural 17-year cycle of life, and not a disaster sent by the gods. Still, whatever their source, the insects ate all the food and the people began to starve. Motecuhzoma had to feed his people from the royal granaries, where grain was stored. To prevent such an event from happening again, many people were sacrificed on the Aztecs' temple altars.

More disasters followed. In 1449, heavy rains and hail caused the water level of Lake Texcoco to rise. The flooding filled the streets of Tenochtitlan with mud. Hail destroyed many of the crops, while other fields and *chinampas* lay under water. Nezahualcoyotl came to Motecuhzoma's aid, and the pair built a nine-mile-long dike (a wall built to prevent flooding) that held back the rising water and reduced the amount of salt in the water. This made farming easier.

The following year, frosts killed the crops. That meant for several years the farmers had not produced enough food to feed the people. The royal granaries were nearly empty, and, with nearly 1 million people to feed, the situation became desperate. Then, after the floods, the Aztecs went through a drought (a long period with no rain). It was so hard to make a living that many people sold themselves into slavery. This was not always a solution, though, since so little food was available that even the wealthy went hungry.

Montezuma or Motecuhzoma?

Nearly all the Aztec names in this book can be spelled in more than one way. That is because the Aztecs did not have an alphabet. The history of the Aztecs was passed on orally or through writing using glyphs. Because each glyph is a symbol for a whole word, Aztec writing does not offer clues to how those words were pronounced.

When the Spanish arrived, they wrote down the Aztec names they heard using Spanish letters and Spanish pronunciations. Not everyone heard the words pronounced the same way, so they came up with different spellings.

Motecuhzoma is probably the most difficult name of them all. In different places, one might find Montezuma, Moctezuma, Motecuhzoma, or Mutezuma. Today, scholars who study the Aztecs and the Nahuatl language they spoke prefer Motecuhzoma. That is the version used in this book.

A Delicate Balance

With their military success, the Aztecs turned themselves into an imperial power. (*Imperial* refers to an empire and its actions.) But that power did not mean others liked or respected them. In the same way that the Aztecs hated the Tepanecs, the peoples who were forced to pay tribute to the Aztecs hated them. The Aztecs found themselves in a difficult position. If they were too demanding, their subjects would rebel. If they were too easygoing, their subjects would ignore Aztec demands. This problem remained a concern for future Aztec *tlatoque*.

The Aztecs wondered how they could make their gods happy again. A religious ceremony that had once called for the sacrifice of a handful of turkeys or a jaguar now called for the sacrifice of many people. They hoped this human sacrifice would satisfy their gods. The prophecies seemed to be coming true—the world was coming to an end.

The end of the Aztecs' many troubles came in 1454. In that year, Motecuhzoma started to rebuild the Great Temple, the pyramid that included the major temple dedicated to Huitzilopochtli. Also in 1454, the people celebrated the New Fire Ceremony, which took place when the two Aztec calendars began again on the same day. This ceremony began with a period of fasting (not eating). Then, a new fire was lit in the temple and carried around to light fires in the hearths (fireplaces) of the city's people. The hearth was the center of family life, where women cooked food and performed religious rituals. The New Fire Ceremony also included human sacrifices to honor the gods.

Work on the Great Temple required building stone. Since the Aztecs' territory had no suitable building stone, they got it by going to war with people who controlled the best building supplies. Once the Aztecs conquered these other cultures, they took the stone as tribute and the conquered people as labor for the building projects.

The city-state of Chalco, about 20 miles from Tenochtitlan, was known for its building stone. It was not yet part of the empire, but the Aztec army quickly changed that. Human sacrifice to Huitzilopochtli was also part of Motecuhzoma's military strategy. Captives from Chalco were marched to Tenochtitlan and sacrificed. The Aztecs now had plenty of stone available for Huitzilopochtli's temple.

AFTER MOTECUHZOMA

Motecuhzoma died in 1468, and the council of elders met to choose a new *tlatoani*. They decided on Motecuhzoma's brilliant advisor, Tlacaelel. But he refused the job. Instead, he suggested Motecuhzoma's son Axayacatl (r. 1469–1481). This was an unusual choice, because Axayacatl was young and untried in war. But Tlacaelel had a lot of influence, and Axayacatl became *tlatoani*.

From the beginning of his rule, Axayacatl faced some difficult problems. The first was a rebellion in the neighboring market city of Tlatelolco. That city had become wealthy because it was a major trading site. The people of Tlatelolco had worked hard for their wealth and resented having to pay tribute to the capital city. Before disagreements broke out into warfare, Axayacatl tried a popular solution: He married his sister to the lord of Tlatelolco. Marriage was a common way to end disputes, but this marriage did not solve the problem. Instead, it created a new one: The bridegroom did not like his bride and treated her badly.

IN THEIR OWN WORDS

The Search for Chicomoztoc

In the 16th century, Spanish priest Diego Durán wrote about Motecuhzoma's decision to seek the Place of the Seven Caves. Here is part of Durán's history. At this point in the story, the sorcerers have found Coatlicue, the god's mother, and tell her about the wealth of the Aztec Empire.

We wish you to know that Motecuhzoma now rules over the great city of Mexico-Tenochtitlan. . . . [T]he city is free, is prosperous. Roads have been opened to the coast, to the sea, to all the land, and these are safe. Tenochtitlan is now the mistress, the princess, the leader and queen of all the cities, all of which pay obedience to her. For now the Aztecs have found the mines of gold and silver and precious stones; they have discovered the home of rich feathers. . . . Motecuhzoma sends you these gifts, which are part of the wealth of your magnificent son Huitzilopochtli and which the king [with Huitzilopochtli's help] has won. . . .

(Source: Durán, Diego. *The History of the Indies of New Spain.* Translated by Doris Heyden. Norman, Okla.: University of Oklahoma Press, 1994.)

Motecuhzoma sent a group of sorcerers to find the Aztec goddess Coatlicue (shown here), the mother of the god Huitzilopochtli.

No one knows for sure what the Temple of Huitzilopochtli really looked like, but this 1722 engraving offers one possible design.

Axayacatl now had only one choice to keep Tlatelolco in line. He sent troops to block all roads leading to the city. His men then attacked and took over the marketplace. Tlatelolco's ruler hid in the temple, where Axayacatl found and killed him. Axayacatl's men destroyed the temple, looted the city, and killed many of the inhabitants.

Axayacatl was thrilled by the success of his first battle. He decided he would test his abilities by expanding his empire to include the more powerful Tarascans—the main rivals of the Aztecs in the west. They lived in and around Lake Patzcuaro. Their main city was Tzintzuntzan almost directly west of Tenochtitlan.

Like the Aztecs, the Tarascans were a military power that expanded by conquering other groups. As a result of their expansion, they controlled areas that produced honey, cotton, feathers, salt, gold, and copper—items the Aztecs wanted. Forty thousand Aztec warriors marched toward the Tarascan city. They set up camp and sent ambassadors to meet with the Tarascan military leaders.

The Aztec ambassadors told the Tarascans that if they did not accept Aztec rule, they would be destroyed in battle. The Tarascans ignored the warning and attacked the Aztecs. The Tarascans had better weapons and were highly skilled warriors. They soon had the Aztecs running in retreat. The Aztecs tried to recover from the loss by launching a sneak attack on the Tarascan military camp. The Tarascans were not fooled and defeated the Aztecs again. When the Aztecs returned to Tenochtitlan, fewer than 2,000 warriors had survived.

Axayacatl had lost a major battle, but he remained *tlatoani*. His officials continued to collect tribute from the nine regions under the *tlatoani's* control. Then, there was a major shift in the balance of power among the three members of the Triple Alliance. In 1472, Nezahualcoyotl, the king of Texcoco, died. Texcoco was left without a strong ruler, and Axayacatl increased his power and the amount of tribute he collected. The Aztec *tlatoani's* wealth grew enormously. He had a special treasure chamber hidden in his palace where he stored his personal gold, silver, gems, feathers, jewelry, and fine cloth.

Nine years after Nezahualcoyotl died, Axayacatl became sick and also died. His brother Tizoc (r. 1481–1486) became *tlatoani*, but he was an extremely poor choice. He was a terrible military leader, and his first venture into war was a bitter disappointment.

In 1481, Tizoc led his troops in his first war as *tlatoani.* They fought the Otomi at Metztitlan. The adventure cost the lives of more than 300 warriors and they brought home only about 30 or 40 prisoners. This, by Aztec standards, was a humiliating defeat.

Tizoc lasted only five years as *tlatoani* and accomplished very little. He died mysteriously and may have been poisoned. Certainly, everyone was relieved when his more capable brother, Ahuitzotl (r. 1486–1502), assumed power.

Powerful Names

In Aztec times, children got their formal name from the official day of their birth according to the sacred or religious calendar. This calendar had 260 days. The name would be a number and a day name, such as 7 Rain. However, since there were only 260 days in the calendar, there were only 260 formal names. With thousands of people, too many people shared the same formal name.

So most Aztecs were known by a nickname. These names, much like the names of native people throughout the Americas, were based on the characteristics of a person, animals, birds, flowers, and even clothing. For example, a person might be called Shining Hummingbird, Maize Flower, or River Woman.

The *tlatoque* also had nicknames. Ahuitzotl means the "water beast," Chimalpopoca means "smoking shield," Itzcoatl means "obsidian serpent," and Motecuhzoma Ilhuicamina means "angry lord who shoots arrows at the sky." These were powerful names for powerful men.

A BRILLIANT MILITARY LEADER

Ahuitzotl began his reign in 1486. Unlike his brother, Ahuitzotl had a brilliant military mind. As soon as he took office, he began planning a campaign of wars to expand the Aztec Empire. Ahuitzotl was adding a new layer to the top of the Great Temple, to make it even taller. The celebration of its completion would be marked by a magnificent sacrifice, and the Aztecs needed to collect a sufficient number of captives.

No one knows how many people were sacrificed in the four-day celebration for Huitzilopochtli's temple. The number may have been in the thousands. So many prisoners of war were sacrificed that the event was the bloodiest celebration the Aztecs ever had.

War and Human Sacrifice

There are stories of the Aztecs sacrificing hundreds and even thousands of people a year, but these stories are exaggerated. Some were told by the conquering Spanish as a way to justify their own violence in taking over Aztec lands. Some were told by the Aztecs themselves to glorify their ancestors.

But when historians look at the most reliable, most specific descriptions of Aztec rituals and actually count the number of human sacrifices they demanded, the number is in the dozens per year. Occasionally, special events were observed with extra sacrifices. Ahuitzotl's temple dedication in 1487 is one famous example. But there is no evidence for the high numbers of sacrifices regularly mentioned in some accounts.

Still, human sacrifice was a major focus of Aztec state rituals. Warfare was conducted so that soldiers were captured alive for sacrifice. (This meant there were much fewer deaths in war than in European warfare of the time.) This practice has lead to stories that the Aztecs made war with the purpose of capturing people for sacrifice. Capturing victims for sacrifice was one of the many ways they justified their warfare. But the Aztecs also expanded their empire to gain access to the riches of their neighbors: cotton, chocolate, jade, quetzal feathers, turquoise, building stone, and other items of value.

In this way, their wars of expansion were very similar to the later conquests of the Spanish. And they were similar in another way, too. The Aztecs and the Spanish were both motivated by a desire for power and glory. They assumed wealth was their well-deserved reward for their military success.

Next, Ahuitzotl turned his attention to unconquered lands surrounding the Aztec Empire. Between 1491 and 1495, the Aztecs brought the region of Oaxaca fully under their rule. The defeated peoples there included the Zapotec. To the west and south of Tenochtitlan, Ahuitzotl took control of Acapulco, on the Pacific Ocean, and the prized region of Soconusco, where cacao beans (which are used to make chocolate) grew. Gold and cotton also poured in as tribute from newly dominated regions.

By this time, the empire of the Triple Alliance had expanded so far that the three city-states lost their ability to control the people under their rule. The burden of constant taxing and providing young men to

The Aztec leader Ahuitzotl carried this featherwork shield. It shows a mighty beast holding a knife between its teeth.

Tenochtitlan Rebuilt

In the early 1500s, a flood poured through Tenochtitlan, destroying many homes, farm plots, and public buildings. The Aztecs offered sacrifices to please their gods and make the waters retreat. As the water levels lowered, the Aztecs saw how badly their city had been damaged. Ahuitzotl immediately ordered that the city be rebuilt.

Stonemasons (people who work with building stone), carpenters, and other craftspeople arrived in Tenochtitlan. They built magnificent palaces that were surrounded by plazas, open streets, and gardens. The dikes that held back the water were made stronger so that flooding would not damage the city again. The city that was nearing its 200th birthday took on a new look.

fight in the army was heavy for those who had been conquered. They believed that the Aztecs had bled their homelands dry so that rulers in Tenochtitlan, Texcoco, and Tlacopan could sit on their jaguar-skin thrones wearing fine clothes and jewelry.

When the Aztecs conquered a people, they usually left the local ruler in place. That ruler became responsible to the leaders of the Triple Alliance. He collected tribute and sent it on to the capital cities. He administered Aztec laws and arranged for young men to serve in the military. In return, the Triple Alliance offered the region protection from outside invasion, a sense of security, and a large trading network.

There was no way for the Aztecs to actually control all the people in the lands they had conquered. They simply had too few warriors and officials to enforce their rule. Their success lay in the ever-present threat of punishment for any rebellion and in the willingness of the local leaders to go along with Aztec wishes.

The Aztec expansion created a never-ending cycle that eventually led to their destruction. They sought more wealth, and that meant they needed to conquer more people. The cost of clothing, arming, and feeding an army, as well as supplying soldiers, put more demands on the conquered people. The endless need for more tribute to pay for the army was a terrible burden that could only be completely filled by conquering still more people. The Aztec Empire under Ahuitzotl grew, but so did its problems.

ANOTHER MOTECUHZOMA

The next *tlatoani* was Motecuhzoma II (r. 1502–1520), who was also known as Motecuhzoma Xocoyotzin—Motecuhzoma the Younger. This distinguished him from his great-grandfather, Motecuhzoma Ilhuicamina.

Motecuhzoma II's father, another Axayacatl (dates unknown), died when his son was 1 year old. Motecuhzoma II was raised in the royal household, studied to be a priest, and knew a great deal about the Aztec religion. He was in his early 20s when Ahuitzotl died.

The new, young *tlatoani* was a gifted leader. He personally led his armies in 43 military victories. But Motecuhzoma II was not just a warrior. He built a double aqueduct to deliver more fresh water to Tenochtitlan. At times, he sneaked into the city wearing a disguise to discover if his latest orders were being carried out. In disguise, he offered bribes to the city judges to find out if any were dishonest. He wanted the Aztecs to have an efficient, honest legal system.

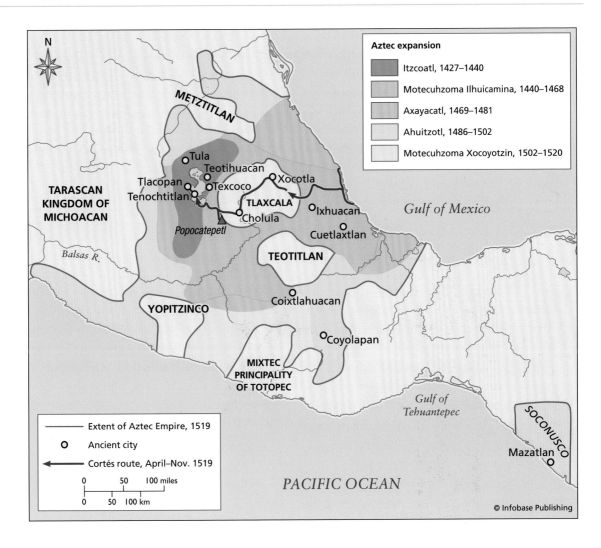

Aztec expansion

- Itzcoatl, 1427–1440
- Motecuhzoma Ilhuicamina, 1440–1468
- Axayacatl, 1469–1481
- Ahuitzotl, 1486–1502
- Motecuhzoma Xocoyotzin, 1502–1520

—— Extent of Aztec Empire, 1519

O Ancient city

◄—— Cortés route, April–Nov. 1519

0   50   100 miles
0   50   100 km

Motecuhzoma II believed that it was important to set nobles apart from commoners (ordinary people). He introduced laws about what clothing people were allowed to wear and the size of their houses. Only nobles were allowed to wear cotton, and only certain nobles could wear red or purple. Nobles could live in two-story homes; commoners could not.

To make sure that members of the royal court were loyal to him, Motecuhzoma II removed from office anyone he distrusted and filled palace jobs with people close to him. He also removed servants who had served previous *tlatoque*. He won the loyalty of leaders from the

Throughout the 14th and early 15th centuries, Aztec rulers accumulated more territory for their empire. This map shows the Aztec Empire at its height, before the arrival of the Spanish in 1520.

provinces by giving palace jobs to their sons. He thought rebellious leaders would think twice before attacking the city where their sons lived and worked.

Motecuhzoma II's palace had no equal. The grand home was basically a square. Inside was a central plaza that featured lush gardens and peaceful courtyards and fishponds. The *tlatoani* also had a zoo, complete with jaguars, coyotes, and snakes. The sprawling stone building constructed around the plaza had more than 300 rooms. The Aztecs bathed daily, and the palace had more than 100 bathing rooms

IN THEIR OWN WORDS

Two Views of Motecuhzoma II

The Aztecs and the Spanish regarded Motecuhzoma II in very different ways. A description from the Codex Mendoza focuses on his qualities as a great leader. The *Codex Mendoza* was written about 20 years after the Spanish conquest by Aztec speakers of Nahuatl. It contains a history of the Aztec rulers and their conquests, a list of the tribute paid by the conquered peoples, and a description of daily Aztec life.

It was most likely commissioned by a Spanish governor named Antonio de Mendoza (1495–1552) to give to Charles V, the king of Spain. The document is in Aztec hieroglyphs with Spanish explanations and commentary. This is some of what it said about Motecuhzoma II.

Motecuhzoma was by nature wise, an astrologer, a philosopher, and skilled in all the arts, civil as well as military. His subjects greatly respected him because of his gravity, demeanor, and power; none of his predecessors, in comparison, could approach his great state and majesty.

The Spanish were interested in very different aspects of the *tlatoani.* Bernal Díaz del Castillo (ca. 1492–ca. 1581), a Spanish priest who traveled with the invading Spanish, focused on Motecuhzoma II's appearance.

The Great Montezuma was about 40 years old, of good height and well proportioned, slender and spare of flesh, not very swarthy, but of the natural colour and shade of an Indian. He did not wear his hair long, but so as just to cover his ears, his scanty black beard was well shaped and thin. His face was somewhat long, but cheerful, and he had good eyes and showed in his appearance and manner both tenderness and, when necessary, gravity. He was very neat and clean and bathed once every day in the afternoon.

(Source: McNeill, William, Sr., ed. *The Berkshire Encyclopedia of World History,* Vol. 3. Great Barrington, Mass.: Berkshire Publishing Group, 2005. Available online. URL: http://drs.asu.edu/fedora/get/asulib:144831/PDF-1. Accessed October 15, 2008; and Díaz del Castillo, Bernal. *The Discovery and Conquest of Mexico.* Cambridge, Mass.: Da Capo Press, 2004.)

and steambaths. The two-story building needed so many rooms and baths because the royal household included several main wives and a number of secondary wives. Also in the palace were the *tlatoani*'s children, servants, and guards.

There were libraries to store government documents and music rooms for entertainment. Bustling kitchens served up meals in sprawling dining halls, feeding guests on venison (deer meat), turkey, fish, wild ducks and geese, and the ever-present dishes made from maize. Honored guests were served roasted agave worms with a sauce made from avocados and red chilies. The *tlatoani* loved chocolate, which was often served as a drink spiced with chili peppers.

The palace was not just the royal home. It was also a business office, much as the White House in Washington, D.C., serves as both the U.S. president's home and office. Included in the palace were apartments for many nobles. Judges and military leaders lived under the *tlatoani*'s watchful eye.

Thanks to years of conquest and tribute, Motecuhzoma II was able to lead a good life in his palace. Some of his subjects might have complained about the tribute they paid, but they still feared the power of the Triple Alliance. Motecuhzoma II's comfortable life, however, took a dramatic turn in 1519, with the arrival of foreigners from across the ocean.

 CONNECTIONS

Agave and Its "Worms"

The worms Motecuhzoma II served his guests were not worms at all. They were larvae, or undeveloped insects, that live near agave plants. Agave is commonly called the century plant or maguey.

The Aztecs believed that agave was a sacred gift from the gods. They used the juice to make *pulque,* an alcoholic beverage. They ate parts of the plant, and they also used it to make pens, nails, sewing needles, and thread. The Aztecs wove the agave fiber into cloth worn by all commoners.

Today, agave is used to make the alcoholic beverages tequila and mezcal. The agave "worms" once roasted for food are put into bottles of mezcal. The worms are also still served in some restaurants in Mexico.

ycpolinhq̃ mexica

CHAPTER 3

THE SPANISH CONQUEST

THERE ARE TWO SIDES TO EVERY STORY, AND THE CONFLICT between the Aztecs and the Spanish is no different. From the Aztec viewpoint, the Spanish were brutal invaders who showed no respect for their leaders, their religion, and their customs. The Aztecs could not understand the Spanish greed for gold and silver. They thought the Spanish were dirty, since bathing was not popular among Europeans at the time.

From the Spanish point of view, the Aztecs were uncivilized and unchristian. They sacrificed human beings and worshipped false gods. The Spanish believed they worshipped the only true god, Jesus Christ, and wanted to convert the Aztecs to their faith. The gold, silver, and other precious items they took were, they believed, their reward for doing this good work.

The Spanish who came to the New World were known as conquistadors, the Spanish word for "conquerors." They were soldiers and adventurers seeking glory and wealth, while also providing a service for their king. The Spanish king hoped to spread the Roman Catholic faith, gain new lands, and acquire wealth.

The Spanish interest in the Valley of Mexico began with a conquistador named Juan de Grijalva (ca. 1489–1527), who arrived in Cuba in 1511. In April 1518, Grijalva set sail from Cuba, heading west. He traveled the coast of Mexico, stopping at small villages (the people he met were not Aztecs). The Spanish received gifts, which they brought back to Diego Velásquez (ca. 1465–1522), the governor of Cuba. The gifts amounted to a small treasure: about $4,000 worth of gold and more than 600 axes made of copper.

OPPOSITE
This 16th-century illustration shows the fateful meeting between Spanish explorers (seated with headdress) and Aztec people.

Old and New World

Old World and New World were terms once used by Europeans who were exploring the world. The Old World refers to Europe. The New World refers to North and South America—an area of the world that was new to Europeans.

Velásquez was pleased with the gifts and anxious to send representatives to the Yucatan Peninsula, the part of southeastern Mexico that juts out into the Gulf Mexico. (Today the region includes Belize and part of Guatemala.) This area was inhabited by the Maya people.

The governor wanted to see exactly how much wealth he could collect for the Spanish king, Charles V (1500–1558). The king received 20 percent (known as the "royal fifth") of any riches found in the New World. But the governor, his representatives, and any men taking part in an expedition received a share of the remaining 80 percent. The possibility of becoming rich encouraged men to take part in dangerous expeditions.

THE CORTÉS EXPEDITION

In the fall of 1518, Velásquez agreed to give Spanish conquistador Hernán Cortés (1485–1547) two or three ships to use for a new expedition to the Yucatan Peninsula. Raising more money on his own, in 1519 Cortés set sail from Cuba with 11 ships, 500 men, horses, and provisions.

With such a large force, Cortés had gone beyond Velásquez's orders. Cortés's expedition was supposed to be an exploratory mission, aimed at checking out possibilities for future conquest. Now Velásquez feared Cortés would try to conquer territory for himself. He sent an order to remove Cortés as commander. Cortés, however, decided to press on. He sailed from the Cuban capital of Santiago to the ports of Trinidad and Havana, where he took on more supplies. He then ignored Velásquez's order to stay in port and left for Mexico.

The trip from Cuba to Mexico's Yucatan Peninsula was a short 120 miles. Cortés dropped anchor and went ashore. His fleet's first stop was the island of Cozumel (Maya for "island of the swallows"), off the eastern coast of the peninsula. The local Maya people watched the ships sail in and the soldiers come ashore, and hid in the surrounding woods.

Cortés and his men looted the town, destroyed statues of the local gods, and put up a Christian cross. After searching the woods and rounding up the local people, Cortés found one man who spoke Spanish. The man told Cortés there were "bearded men" who lived six days journey from Cozumel.

Cortés knew that some Spanish men had been shipwrecked eight years ago, and hoped the "bearded men" might be the survivors of that wreck. Eventually, he found one of them, Gerónimo de Aguilar (ca. 1489–1531). This was an incredible stroke of luck. Aguilar had learned Maya and became Cortés's translator.

A woman named Malintzin (ca. 1501–ca. 1550) also joined Cortés's expedition. Malintzin was a central Mexican woman who had been sold into slavery to the Maya. Little is know about her life before she joined Cortés's expedition, though some sources say she was the daughter of a chief who lived near the Tabasco River in southeastern Mexico.

This woman spoke both Maya and Nahuatl, which enabled her to translate for Cortés. The first conversations Cortés had with Aztec messengers and leaders went through two translations: Cortés spoke

Hernán Cortés

Hernán Cortés was born in 1485 in Medellín, a poor village in the rugged region of Estremadura, Spain. He was a sickly child, but grew into a strong man. His parents arranged for him to study the law, but Cortés was interested only in becoming a soldier.

At the age of 18, Cortés sailed for Hispaniola, an island in the West Indies. Several years later, Cortés left Hispaniola for Cuba, where he became involved in raising cattle and shipping. Cortés was the first European to raise cattle in Cuba, but the life of a farmer did not interest him. He wanted gold and riches.

As soon as he heard that Juan de Grijalva had sailed to a land called Mexico and found gold there, Cortés was anxious to leave Cuba. He set sail for Mexico in 1519, and eventually made history by conquering the powerful Aztec Empire.

A statue of Hernán Cortés stands in Medillin, Spain.

IN THEIR OWN WORDS

Cortés Claims the Land for Spain

In his history of the Cortés expedition, *The Discovery and Conquest of Mexico*, Spanish priest Bernal Díaz del Castillo said the first thing Cortés did when he came ashore in Cozumel was declare that the lands he found in Mexico now belonged to the Spanish king. He described the ceremony in which Cortés made this claim.

> There and then Cortés took possession of that land for His Majesty, performing the act in His Majesty's name. It was done in this way; he drew his sword and as a sign of possession made three cuts in a huge tree called a CIBA, which stood in the court of that great square, and cried that if any person should raise objection, that he would defend the right with the sword and shield which he held in his hands.

(Source: Díaz del Castillo, Bernal. *The Discovery and Conquest of Mexico.* Cambridge, Mass.: Da Capo Press, 2004.)

to Aguilar in Spanish, Aguilar spoke to Malintzin in Maya, and Malintzin spoke to the Aztecs in Nahuatl. Traveling with the Spanish, she quickly learned their language and eventually Cortés did not need Aguilar as a translator. She later played an important role for Cortés, helping him recruit Nahuatl-speaking allies.

MOTECUHZOMA II SENDS MESSENGERS

Word was sent to Motecuhzoma II that strangers had arrived in his land. He was concerned and curious and wanted to find out more. So he immediately sent messengers to meet with them. Cortés had moved along the coast to an area controlled by the Totonacs. This was where Motecuhzoma II's messengers first met Cortés.

The messengers were under orders to feed the guests, give them gifts, and basically check them out. The Aztecs arrived dressed for an event of great importance. They presented the Spanish with items the Aztecs treasured: a serpent mask inlaid with turquoise, a garment made of feathers, necklaces of shells, and items made of gold. The Spanish had no interest in the feathers and shells, but they were delighted to see the gold.

Cortés decided to put on a show that would impress his hosts. He had his men ride along the beach in full armor, waving their swords. He fired his cannon, which scared the Aztecs because they had no knowledge of gunpowder. He told the Aztecs that in the morning they would have hand-to-hand combat as a test of strength. He gave them swords, spears, and leather shields. "It will take place very early, at daybreak. We are going to fight each other in pairs, and in this way we will learn the truth. We will see who falls to the ground" (quoted in *The Aztec Account of the Spanish Conquest of Mexico*).

The messengers were very confused. They had followed their customs and the orders of their ruler. They expected the Spanish to offer friendship in return. But it seemed the Spanish strangers were not satisfied. They had challenged the Aztec messengers to combat. They were messengers, not warriors. It would have been very inappropriate for them to fight the Spanish, and they did not.

The Incredible Life of Gerónimo de Aguilar

In 1511, a Spanish sailing ship ran aground in the shallow water off Jamaica. The ship sank and the 20 or so crew members made it into a lifeboat. They drifted on the ocean for 13 days. They had no provisions, and nearly half died before winds and current carried them to the coast of the Yucatan Peninsula.

Once ashore, the local Maya people captured them and prepared to sacrifice them at an upcoming festival. Two of them, Gerónimo de Aguilar and Gonzalo Guerrero (dates unknown), escaped just before the festival and fled.

Once again they were captured, but this time it was by a rival chief. According to Aguilar and Guerrero, he treated them well, although he also made them his slaves.

These shipwrecked Spanish brought with them a host of European diseases, including influenza, measles, smallpox, and typhus. A terrible plague of disease swept through the village where Aguilar and Guerrero lived. They were the only survivors. Aguilar struck out in search of other Spanish people, but Guerrero decided to live among the Maya.

When the Maya Hernán Cortés met told him about some "bearded men," Cortés decided to send them a letter by messenger. In the letter, Cortés set a meeting time. But the time to meet came and went. Cortés assumed his letter had never been delivered, so he sailed on. He did not get far before one of his ships began leaking and Cortés ordered the fleet back to Cozumel for repairs.

While the repairs were being done, a man paddling a canoe approached the fleet. His clothes were so tattered that he was nearly naked. The canoe paddler was Aguilar.

Decorative treasures such as this double-headed snake ornament were part of the horde of gifts presented by the Aztecs to Cortés.

When the messengers returned to Tenochtitlan, they reported on what had happened. They told Motecuhzoma II about the cannon. They described the Spanish armor and horses, which they thought were large deer. The Aztecs had never seen horses before. To them, these were deer that grew so big they could carry men on their backs.

The strangers also looked unlike any people the Aztecs knew. They had light skin and some had yellow hair. Their hair was curly. Their beards were long and bushy. The Aztecs had darker skin, straight, dark hair, and very light beards that they kept shaved.

The Aztec army was so powerful that Motecuhzoma II believed he had nothing to fear. But he did want to know more about these strangers. Motecuhzoma II immediately sent more men to speak with the Spanish. This group consisted of warriors, prophets, and wizards. They brought with them a group of captives to be sacrificed, just in case the strangers were gods.

The Spanish watched the captives being sacrificed in horror. Dishes were cooked and served, and sprinkled with the blood of the scarified victims. The Spanish refused to eat the feast put before them. The Aztecs now knew that the strangers were not gods, because their gods would have welcomed these offerings. The Spanish were clearly men. But the Aztecs still did not know what these strangers from far away intended to do in their lands.

MAKING ALLIANCES

Cortés arrived at a time when the Aztec Empire was stretched so far that it could not realistically control all its territory. Subject peoples were paying an increasingly heavy burden in tribute and warriors. And the Triple Alliance was weakening. Many of the people under Aztec control were looking for a way to break free.

While they were on the coast, Cortés and his men were in the land of the Totonac. These people were part of the Aztec Empire and resented the tribute they had to pay. Cortés convinced them to become his allies against the Aztecs. Other subject peoples, also angry after long years of domination by the Aztecs, would later join Cortés, giving him thousands of allies.

Cortés also used violence to secure allies. At times, he raided villages while the people were asleep and committed terrible acts of war, such as chopping off people's hands. The native peoples had never seen such brutal warfare. The cruelty of the Spanish convinced some of the Native Americans that it was better to join the strangers than to fight them.

Among the Totonac, Cortés learned about Tenochtitlan and its great wealth. The riches of the city were only 200 miles away, and he wanted them. But there were rumblings among his crew. Some wanted to head back to Cuba to tell Governor Velásquez what they had found. Cortés had no intention of allowing them to do so, because he did not want other men to follow him and share in the great wealth of the Aztecs. To prevent a rebellion among his men, he sank their ships. Then he turned west and began the long march inland.

As they traveled, the Spanish faced the Otomi in battle. Once again, the difference between native and Spanish customs favored the Spanish. The Otomi had rituals that had to be observed before a battle. Among the peoples of Central America, these rituals were respected and one army would not attack another while they were practicing their pre-battle ritual. But the Spanish did not know about these customs and probably would not have cared even if they had known. They slaughtered the Otomi as they were preparing for the battle. News of the Spanish victory spread quickly.

When the Spanish met the Tlaxcalans, they found an ally. The lords of Tlaxcala knew that the Otomi were excellent warriors and that the Spanish had slaughtered them. Not wanting to face a

Preaching Christianity

The Spanish felt it was their duty to preach about Christianity to anyone who was not Roman Catholic. When meeting the native peoples of the New World, they felt obliged to convert them to the Catholic faith. In letters Cortés sent home, he described one way this was done.

He wrote, "The captain reproved them for their evil practice of worshipping their idols and gods, and made them understand how they must come to the knowledge of our Holy Faith; and he left them a wooden cross planted on a height, with which they were well pleased . . . " (quoted in Hernán Cortés, *Letters from Mexico*).

This excerpt shows how little respect the Spanish had for the religions of the native peoples they met. They regarded these religions as evil and wrong. The part about the local people being well pleased with the wooden cross was probably an exaggeration.

CONNECTIONS

Spanish Horses

Several million years ago, ancestors of today's horses roamed North America. Eventually they became extinct, so the Aztecs and the other peoples of the New World had never seen these powerful, fast animals. All the horses that eventually ended up in North and South America were descendants of the horses the Spanish brought.

The horse would play an important role in the culture of Native American groups in Mexico and what became the U.S. Southwest and the Great Plains. The Native Americans used the horses in warfare, just as the Spanish did. Parts of Mexico developed an economy based on ranching, and the first *vaqueros*, or cowboys, emerged there. Many of the first Mexican cowboys were mestizo—people of mixed Spanish and Native American ancestry.

Today, a type of horse first bred in Mexico is called the Azteca. The breeders wanted a horse similar to the ones that came from Spain in the 16th century.

similar fate, the Tlaxcalans welcomed the invaders. They provided information about the trip to Tenochtitlan and honored their Spanish guests in every way.

At this time the Tlaxcalans were enemies of Cholula, and decided to use their alliance with the Spanish to pursue their own goals. They told Cortés that Cholula was an evil city and that its people were allies of the Aztecs. The Spanish headed for Cholula ready for battle.

Word was sent to Cholula that the Tlaxcalans and their friends came in peace. The warriors of Cholula welcomed the Tlaxcalans and the men with them as friends. They met in the main plaza without armor or weapons. The Spanish then blocked off the exits from the plaza and began killing the Cholultecas. They stabbed them and pierced them with their spears. The Spanish entered the temple and destroyed the idol of Quetzalcoatl. (An idol is an image of a god that is believed to be sacred.)

Word of the Cholulteca defeat reached the Aztecs. They had no idea that the Cholultecas had been tricked by the Tlaxcalans and the Spanish. The Aztecs believed that the Spanish had met and beaten the Cholultecas in a fair battle, as the Aztecs did when they fought their enemies. When the Aztecs went to war, they followed the accepted customs of their people. At times, they would even send weapons to their enemies to make sure the fight was fair. The Aztecs assumed the Spanish waged war the same way. If they defeated the Cholultecas, these strangers must possess a powerful army.

At that point, Motecuhzoma II sent some warriors to turn back the Spanish and their allies as they approached Tenochtitlan. But the ruler

The temple at Cholula was the site of a massacre of native peoples by Cortés.

of the mighty Aztec Empire simply did not realize the extent of the threat, and his efforts were too little.

THE SPANISH ARRIVE IN TENOCHTITLAN

The Aztecs sent even more gifts, and this time the Spanish liked them better. They included items made of gold and of quetzal feathers. With all these gifts, the Aztecs were trying to impress the Spanish. They wanted the Spanish to see the great power the Aztecs had and make them realize they could not compete with the Aztec army. If the Spanish feared the Aztecs, perhaps they would leave.

The Spanish, though, did not understand the meaning of these gifts. They thought the gifts meant to please them, when in fact, they were subtle threats. And once the Spanish had seen the gold, they were determined to march on.

This was another way that the Aztecs and the Spanish differed. The Aztecs could not understand the interest the Spanish had in gold. To the Aztecs, gold was valuable only for the beautiful things that could be made from it. The Aztecs did not have an economy based on money—goods were exchanged by trading one item of value for

IN THEIR OWN WORDS

Spreading the News of Destruction

This is how the Spanish described their attack on Cholula and the terror that followed.

When Cholula had been stormed and destroyed, and a great host of people killed and plundered, our armies marched forward again, causing terror wherever they went, until the news of the destruction spread through the whole land. The people were astonished to hear such strange reports, and to learn how the Cholultecas were defeated and slain in so short a time, and how their idol Quetzalcoatl had not served them in any way.

(Source: Léon-Portilla, Miguel. *The Broken Spears: The Aztec Account of the Conquest of Mexico.* Boston: Beacon Press, 1990.)

another. The Aztecs did not have gold coins; they had works of art and jewelry.

The Aztecs also highly valued quetzal feathers, cacao beans, and shells. To the Spanish, gold was the most valuable thing in the world. They did not treasure it for its beauty, but for its value as money. They did not appreciate the works of art given to them. Once the Spanish got their hands on gold, they quickly melted the art and jewelry into bars called ingots, which were easier to transport.

Finally, the Spanish arrived in Tenochtitlan, with thousands of Tlaxcalan warriors and other allies by their side. By this time, Cortés had heard much about Motecuhzoma II and Motecuhzoma had heard much about him. The people of Tenochtitlan came out in droves to see the strangers. Gossip and rumors filled the air, as the Spanish marched over the causeway and into the city. People sat in canoes on both sides of the causeway and lined the streets.

Motecuhzoma II met his guests at the gates to the city. The Aztec *tlatoani* wore his finest clothes and jewelry when he met the Spanish conquistador. He sat on a litter, a type of portable couch, and was carried by the nobles of the city. He stepped down from the litter and placed necklaces of gold and precious stones around Cortés's neck. Cortés placed a necklace of pearls and cut glass around the neck of Motecuhzoma, but was held back by two lords when he tried to embrace the *tlatoani*.

Motecuhzoma II reportedly greeted Cortés in a manner that is typical Aztec polite speech. He suggested that the Spanish were welcome to treat the city as if it was their home. But Cortés did not understand the customs of Nahuatl speech-making. He chose to see the speech as meaning the Aztecs were ready to surrender to him and King Charles. He then wrote back to the Spanish king, making it look as if Motecuhzoma II was willing to submit to him. In fact, this was not true. Cortés's mistake was a combination of misunderstanding and exaggeration. He exaggerated because he was already in trouble with Governor Velásquez and hoped he could win the favor of the king.

The Spanish were very interested in what they saw of Tenochtitlan. Cortés described the city as built on an island in a great salt lake. He said that it was as large as Seville, a city in Spain. The layout of the city—half streets on land and half canals—impressed the Spanish. They were also interested in the temples, the palaces, and the thriving market. The Spanish may or may not have noticed that the city was remarkably clean—something that could not be said for Spanish cities in the 1500s. The Aztecs bathed daily and kept their streets and homes clean. The Spanish bathed rarely and cleaned their streets even less often.

While the Spanish were fascinated by everything they saw, they were not impressed with the Aztec religion. Motecuhzoma II arranged for Cortés to visit the Great Temple, the holiest place in Tenochtitlan. The *tlatoani* went with them, and the group went up the 114 steps to the top of the pyramid. Cortés asked to see the Aztec gods, and was shown the many idols that were kept in the temple. Three sacrifices had taken place that day and blood covered the walls. The hearts of the victims burned in front of the idols.

The sights and smells revolted Cortés. He wrote that he told Motecuhzoma II, "I do not understand how such a great Prince and wise man as you are has not come to the conclusion . . . that these idols of yours are not gods, but evil things that are called devils" (quoted in Bernal Díaz del Castillo's *The Discovery and Conquest of Mexico*). Cortés had offended the *tlatoani* in the worst possible way. He even asked if he could place a cross, the symbol of the Roman Catholic Church, in the Aztec temple.

Cortés and his men accepted Motecuhzoma II's invitation to stay at his palace, although they felt nervous about their situation. They were outnumbered and, even with their superior weapons, they knew the Aztecs could easily kill them. Cortés wrote to King Charles that the *tlatoani* was under arrest, but that is very unlikely.

Eventually, though, Motecuhzoma II did come under Cortés's direct control. The constant presence of the Spanish, with their strange and fascinating ways, slowly influenced Motecuhzoma. They began to surround him day and night, and eventually separated him from his lords and priests. Then they used the threat of their superior weapons to take him under their control.

Aztec Markets

The Spanish admired the large, orderly markets of the Aztec cities. After seeing Tlatelolco, Tenochtitlan's sister city, Bernal Díaz del Castillo wrote in *The Discovery and Conquest of Mexico* that "each kind of merchandise was kept by itself and had its fixed place marked out. Let us begin with the dealers in gold, silver, and precious stones, feathers, mantles, and embroidered goods. Then there were other wares consisting of Indian slaves both men and women. . . . In another part there were skins of tigers and lions of otters and jackals, deer and other animals and badgers and mountain cats. . . ."

Under an armed Spanish guard, Motecuhzoma II led the Spanish to the royal treasure room. The invaders ignored the things the Aztecs valued most and collected all the gold. They set fire to the feathers and other items they did not want. The Spanish also went through the royal palace, taking whatever precious stones and items of value they found. Cortés and his men had found the fortunes they had hoped for. Bernal Díaz del Castillo wrote in *The Discovery and Conquest of Mexico*, "When I saw it, I tell you, I was amazed. . . . [I] had never in my whole life seen riches like it before."

Since Cortés and his small force could never directly take over Tenochtitlan, he made a more subtle plan. He wanted to keep Motecuhzoma II as a prisoner in his palace and use him as a puppet. The *tlatoani* would rule the Aztecs in whatever way the Spanish wanted. This plan never worked out, though. As soon as the Aztecs

IN THEIR OWN WORDS

Two Versions of Motecuhzoma's Speech

The Aztecs wrote down their version of the meeting between Cortés and Motecuhzoma II. Here is a modern translation of part of the Aztec *tlatoani*'s greeting.

Our lord, you are weary. The journey has tired you, but now you have arrived on the earth. You have come to your city, Mexico. You have come here to sit on your throne, to sit under its canopy.

The kings who have gone before, your representatives, guarded it and preserved it for your coming. The kings Itzcoatl, Motecuhzoma the Elder, Axayacatl, Tizoc and Ahuitzotl ruled for you in the City of Mexico. The people were protected by their swords and sheltered by their shields.

Do the kings know the destiny of those they left behind, their posterity? If only

they are watching! If only they can see what I see!

No, it is not a dream. I am not walking in my sleep. I am not seeing you in my dreams. . . . I have seen you at last! I have met you face to face! I was in agony for five days, for ten days, with my eyes fixed on the Region of the Mystery. And now you have come out of the clouds and mists to sit on your throne again.

This was foretold by the kings who governed your city, and now it has taken place. You have come back to us; you have come down from the sky. Rest now, and take possession of your royal houses. Welcome to your land, my lords!

Cortés also wrote to King Charles V of Spain, offering his view of what Motecuhzoma II said.

realized Motecuhzoma II was being controlled by the Spanish, they stopped obeying his orders.

A MASSACRE AND A RETREAT

The year 1520 brought problems for Cortés. In the early spring, Governor Velásquez sent troops to arrest him for defying the governor's orders. Cuban troops under the command of Pánfilo de Narváez (ca. 1478–1528) landed on the coast of Mexico, and word quickly arrived in Tenochtitlan that more Spanish had arrived. Cortés put Lieutenant Pedro de Alvarado (ca. 1485–1541) in charge of the city (Alvarado had been on Grijalva's first expedition to Mexico in 1518). Cortés took as many soldiers and allied warriors as he could with him to the coast.

For a long time we have known from the writing of our ancestors that neither I, not any of those who dwell in this land, are natives of it, but foreigners who came from very distant parts; and likewise we know that a chieftain of whom they were all vassals brought our people to this region. And he returned to his native land and after many years came again, by which time all those who had remained were married to native women and had built villages and raised children. And when he wished to lead them away again they would not go, not even admit him as their chief; and so he departed. And we have always held that those who descended from him would come and conquer this land and take us as their vassals. So because of the place from which you claim to come, namely from where the sun rises, and the things you tell us of the great lord or king who sent you here, we believe and are certain that he is our natural lord, especially as you say that he has known of us for some time. So be assured that we will obey you and hold you as our lord in place of that great sovereign of whom you speak; and in this there shall be no offence or betrayal whatsoever. And in all the land that lies in my domain, you may command as you will, for you shall be obeyed; and all that we own is for you to dispose of as you choose. Thus now as you are in your own country and your own house, rest now after the hardships of your journey.

(Source: "An Aztec Account of the Conquest of Mexico." Modern History Sourcebook, Fordham University. Available online. URL: http://www.fordham.edu/halsall/mod/Aztecs1.html. Accessed May 22, 2008; and "Montezuma's Speech," from *"The Fall of* the Aztecs." Conquistadors. Available online. URL: http://www.pbs.org/conquistadors/cortes/cortes_e03.htm. Accessed June 22, 2008.)

Cortés arrived on the coast to confront Narváez. Rather than meet with Narváez and discuss the situation, Cortés chose to attack at night. His men ambushed Narváez, who was surprised at how quickly Cortés defeated him. Those soldiers who survived the ambush joined forces with Cortés.

While Cortés was gone, Alvarado took advantage of his position. By now, Motecuhzoma II was a prisoner of the Spanish. The Aztecs wanted to hold the annual celebration in honor of Huitzilopochtli. The Spanish were interested in watching such a festival even though they were disgusted by Aztec human sacrifices. Representatives from Tenochtitlan went to the palace and asked if they might hold the festival. They got permission to do so.

The celebration required extensive preparations. For example, those participating needed to make a statue of Huitzilopochtli. The local women began grinding seeds. The night before the event, the Aztecs built their model of Huitzilopochtli from a paste made of the ground seeds spread over a stick frame, much like papier-mâché. Artisans dressed the statue with feathers and painted its face. They added gold jewelry, turquoise, and other finery fit for their god. The young warriors prepared to dance and sing, which was one of the most important parts of the ritual.

The festival started with a parade through the main plaza. The people filled the plaza, cheering the warriors who would perform the serpent dance. The people sang and danced. That was when everything went wrong.

Alvarado ordered his men to attack the people in the plaza. The Spanish blocked the gates into the plaza, which prevented people from leaving, and they proceeded to kill as many Aztecs as they could. Alvarado justified the attack by claiming it was a way to prevent the human sacrifices he heard would occur at the ceremony. But it is more likely that he saw it as a convenient opportunity to kill a lot of warriors. The dancing warriors were not armed and could not defend themselves from the Spanish attack.

The Spanish had made a terrible mistake. Up to this point, the Aztecs had been peaceful, even when the Spanish imprisoned their *tlatoani*. But this unexpected act of extreme violence enraged them. Many came running with clubs and spears. A battle began, as the Aztecs attacked with all their power. They outnumbered the Spanish, who quickly retreated to the palace.

When Cortés returned to Tenochtitlan, the situation was desperate. The Spanish fought back, shooting their guns and cannon, but there were simply too many Aztecs. Cortés tried to gain Motecuhzoma II's help to end the fighting and bring peace to the city. Motecuhzoma II told the people to put down their weapons and give up. But by this time, the council of elders had made Motecuhzoma II's brother Cuitlahuac (r. 1520) the *tlatoani*. No one listened to Motecuhzoma II, and the fighting continued. The former *tlatoani* soon died in the raging battle.

Cortés realized that the Spanish needed to leave the city. Rain poured down, aiding his men in their retreat. Just before midnight on July 1, 1520, the Spanish and their Tlaxcalan and other allies tried to sneak away in the middle of the night. But they were seen by the Aztecs, who were familiar with all the roads in the city. The Spanish were caught on the causeway to Tlacopan and surrounded by Aztecs in canoes. The Aztecs let loose a

IN THEIR OWN WORDS

The Death of Motecuhzoma

There are several versions of how Motecuhzoma II died. Here, Cortés presents his view.

> Mutezuma . . . was asked to be taken out onto the roof of the fortress where he might speak to the captains of his people and tell them to end the fighting . . . he received a blow on his head from a stone and the injury was so serious that he died three days later.

Bernal Díaz del Castillo wrote:

> [T]here was such a shower of stones and javelins that Montezuma was hit by three stones, one on the head, another on the arm, and the third on the leg. . . .

And Fernando de Alva Cortés Ixtlilxochilt, the great-great-great-great-grandson of Nezahualcoyotl, offered another version:

> It is said that an Indian killed him with a stone from his sling, but the palace servants declared that the Spanish put him to death by stabbing him in the abdomen with their swords.

Still other Aztecs accounts say the Spanish strangled Motecuhzoma II. Today, no one knows for sure how he died.

(Source: Cortés, Hernán. *Letters from Mexico.* Translated and edited by Anthony Pagden. New Haven, Conn.: Yale University Press, 1986; Idell, Albert, editor and translator. *The Bernal Díaz Chronicles.* Garden City, N.Y.: Dolphin Books, 1956; and Léon-Portilla, Miguel. *The Broken Spears: The Aztec Account of the Conquest of Mexico.* Boston: Beacon Press, 1990.)

storm of arrows. The Spanish fired their cannons, but the Aztecs rowed their canoes in a zigzag pattern to avoid the cannon balls.

When the Spanish and their allies reached the Toltec canal, Aztecs in canoes grabbed the Spanish by the legs and pulled them into the water. They held them underwater until they drowned. Some soldiers threw themselves into the water. Between the heavy armor the Spanish wore and the gold that weighted them down, the soldiers could not swim to safety. The bodies of men and horses floated in the water.

Two-thirds of the fleeing Spanish died, along with nearly 1,000 Tlaxcalan warriors who fought with the Spanish. Cortés wept for the loss of men, horses, and treasure.

The few survivors headed for the safety of Tlaxcala. Most were wounded at least once. With enemies on all sides, the Spanish and their allies had no place to rest. They ate what maize they could scavenge and also cooked and ate the meat of their dead horses. Before they could reach Tlaxcala, though, they had to fight the Aztecs again.

On the plains of Otumba, the two armies met. In a desperate move, Cortés captured one of the Aztec generals. The Spanish were vastly outnumbered, but this bold move caused the Aztecs to retreat. The route to Tlaxcala was open, and the Spanish headed to the home of their greatest allies.

THE SPANISH RETURN

Now the Spanish wanted more than just gold from the Aztecs. They had managed to gain control of Tenochtitlan once, and they wanted it back. They also wanted revenge for the conquistadors who had been killed. At Tlaxcala, the soldiers healed and Cortés built up his army with both Spanish and local allies. Spanish reinforcements arrived from other areas. And, increasingly, the native peoples joined with the Spanish because they felt optimistic that they would be able to defeat the Aztecs.

Back in Tenochtitlan, the people began to think that they had seen the last of the Spanish and breathed a sigh of relief. Then, in September, the Aztecs suffered a terrible blow. Smallpox, brought by the Spanish to all of the New World, raced through the population. Diseases such as smallpox had been present for so long in Europe that many Europeans had been exposed to them and had some immunity against their effects. But the peoples of the New World had never encountered these diseases and had no immunity at all and no medicine to relieve the coughs, fevers, blisters, and sores that came with smallpox.

IN THEIR OWN WORDS

The Great Misery

Bernardino de Sahagún (ca. 1499–1590) was a Spanish priest who was sent to Mexico to convert the native peoples to Christianity. Sahagún eventually learned Nahuatl and collected Aztec writings and conducted interviews in that language. He and his students compiled 12 books from these native sources. Some of the writings were translated into Spanish, but most were not. They are now known as the *Florentine Codex* or *General History of the Things of New Spain*.

This is what the *Florentine Codex* had to say about the smallpox epidemic:

It caused great misery. Some people it covered with pustules, everywhere, the face, the head, the breast, etc. Many indeed perished from it. They could not walk; they could only lie at home in their beds, unable to move, to raise themselves, to stretch out on their sides, or lie face down, or upon their backs. If they stirred they cried out with great pain. Like a covering over them were the pustules.

On some the pustules broke out far apart. They did not cause much suffering, nor did many die of them. Many others were harmed by them on their faces; face and nose were left roughened. Some had their eyes injured by them; they were blinded. Many were crippled by it—though not entirely.

The pestilence lasted through 60 day signs before it diminished.

(Source: "The Fall of the Aztecs." *Conquistadors.* Available online. URL: http://www.pbs.org/conquistadors/cortes/cortes_e03.htm. Accessed June 22, 2008.)

The epidemic lasted for just over two months and left thousands dead. Cuitlahuac may have been one of the victims, although historians are not sure. In any event, he died in 1520 and Motecuhzoma II's nephew Cuauhtemoc (r. 1520–1521) was chosen as *tlatoani*. The young man possessed the bravery needed in a leader during this time of crisis.

Meanwhile, Cortés prepared his counterattack. It had been almost two years since Cortés first arrived in Mexico. The handful of Spanish soldiers who had come on his first expedition had been reinforced by Narváez's surviving men and also by additional ships from Cuba. Cortés's father even sent a shipload of men and supplies from Spain.

Eventually, even long-term allies like the Acolhua, Nezahualcoyotl's people, started splitting away and joining with the Spanish. They thought they were gaining their independence from the Aztec Empire.

They had no idea what they were getting into: 300 years of Spanish colonial rule, impoverishment, and loss of power.

In December 1520, Cortés's troops and allies marched toward the heart of the Aztec Empire. Using native workers, the Spanish had built 12 brigantines (a type of sailing ship) that Cortés planned to use to cross Lake Texcoco. More than 8,000 Native Americans took apart and carried the ships to the lake, then reassembled them. Cortés's plan was to set up a siege. In this military tactic, an army surrounds a city or fort and prevents it from receiving supplies or more troops.

When Cortés arrived, he cut off the island on which Tenochtitlan was built. On May 30, 1521, the Spanish launched the brigantines they had brought in pieces to the shores of Lake Texcoco. They used their ships to attack the Aztecs on the causeways and to stop canoes from crossing the lake to bring supplies. The Spanish cut the flow of fresh water into the city. Cortés knew that a city without food and water could not survive.

IN THEIR OWN WORDS

Broken Bones Littered the Road

In the years after the Spanish invasion, several Aztec poets wrote elegies—poems written for the dead or after a great loss. Here is part of one found in Tlatelolco. It dates to the 1540s or 1550s.

Note the powerful image of shields, which are meant to defend the city, being used in desperation to toast a few worms for a starving person or to protect a crumbling wall.

Thus in our place this happened; we saw it, we will marvel at it. The crying, the pity caused us to suffer exhaustion.

Broken bones littered the road; crushed heads, roofless houses, walls were made red with blood.

Worms crawled through noses in the streets; the house walls were slippery with brains.

The water was dyed red with blood. Thus we went along; we drank the brackish water.

Still, there an adobe foundation, here a well protected with a shield.

Still, in vain someone might toast something on a shield.

We ate tzompantli wood, grass from the salt flats, the adobe bricks, the lizards, mice, bits of dust.

Worms were toasted on a shield; there, on the fire the meat was cooked. They ate it.

(Source: Courtesy of John Frederick Schwaller, translator, copyright 2008, all rights reserved.)

When it became clear that the Spanish were a serious threat, the Aztecs defended themselves fiercely and heroically, and adapted to Spanish styles of fighting. But they were abandoned by their allies and subjects and besieged in Tenochtitlan. They held out as long as they could, with Cuauhtemoc valiantly leading them. But their fresh water and food supplies were cut off and they were starving, drinking salty lake water, and eating worms, mice, weeds, and anything else they could find.

Cortés was amazed by the city of Tenochtitlan and did not want to destroy it. The Spanish wanted to conquer Mexico and then live as noblemen on big estates with the native people working for them and paying tribute to them. But in the end, because the Aztecs refused to surrender, destroying Tenochtitlan was the only way he could conquer it.

The Aztecs held out for 80 days. During that time, Cortés and his troops landed on the southern shore of the island. They fought their way through the city, advancing street by street, meeting heavy resistance. They destroyed entire *calpullis* to prevent Aztec warriors from ambushing them.

Slowly, the whole southern part of the island gave way to the Spanish attack. But conquering the entire island would take more than two months. Finally, Cuauhtemoc realized his people could not win and he surrendered. The historian Alva Ixtilxochitl later wrote, "On the day that Tenochtitlan was taken, the Spanish committed some of the most brutal acts ever inflicted upon the unfortunate people of this land. The cries of the helpless women and children were heart-rending. The Tlaxcalans and other enemies of the Aztecs revenged themselves pitilessly for old offences and robbed them of everything they could find" (quoted in *The Fall of the Aztecs*).

After his defeat, Cuauhtemoc was taken prisoner by Cortés and tortured. The conquistador finally executed Cuauhtemoc in 1525, when he feared the former Aztec *tlatoani* might lead a rebellion against Spanish rule.

THE END OF AN EMPIRE

The fall of Tenochtitlan marked the end of the Aztec Empire. Tlatelolco soon fell as well. The Aztecs still chose their own leaders, but those men had to obey the Spanish. Some rulers who promised loyalty to Spain were allowed to govern their local communities, but they, too, had to answer to Spanish officials.

National Hero

Cuauhtemoc has become a national hero in Mexico for his bravery fighting against a foreign invader. A statue of Cuauhtemoc was put up in Mexico City in 1887, and today boys are sometimes named after him. Some of the more prominent Cuauhtemocs of recent years include the soccer star Cuauhtemoc Blanco (b. 1973) and the political leader Cuauhtemoc Cardenas (b. 1934).

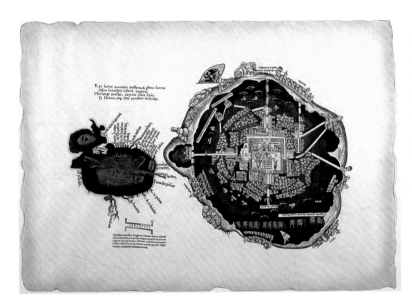

This map, drawn in 1524, shows what Europeans believed the Aztec Empire looked like.

Some high-ranking Spanish men married local noblewomen, because few Spanish women settled in the colony. Even when they did come, those women never married native men. Over time, the mestizo children of the Spanish settlers and native women also took important roles in the society of New Spain—the Spanish name for the former Aztec Empire and other parts of modern-day Mexico.

The gold Cortés craved made its way into the treasury of King Charles and into the pockets of Cortés and his men. Thousands of Spanish moved to Mexico to settle and exploit the land. There was not all that much gold in Mexico, but there was plenty of silver. Eventually silver mining became a major source of wealth for the Spanish, who forced the native people to work long hours under terrible conditions in the silver mines.

With the Spanish conquest, the Roman Catholic Church sent priests as missionaries to convert the native people. Charles V and later Spanish rulers took this effort very seriously. Many Aztecs who wished to become Catholic were allowed to keep their estates, which was a major incentive. Catholicism became the religion of Mexico, as it is to this day.

But the Aztec Catholics did not practice their faith as most Europeans did. The native people who accepted Catholicism adapted it to suit their own religious traditions. They emphasized public rituals, sacred images, and making offerings. Churches were typically built on or near the sites of the old temples, reusing the same building materials and even pieces of statues or whole carvings. Human sacrifice was abandoned with little regret—which showed that it was mainly an activity of the Aztec warrior state.

As more Spanish arrived, they slowly took over all of Mexico and Central America. The land that was once home to great, independent civilizations was now completely under foreign control.

PART·II

SOCIETY AND CULTURE

AZTEC SOCIETY

DAILY LIFE AMONG THE AZTECS

RELIGION, ART, AND SCIENCE

CHAPTER 4

AZTEC SOCIETY

THE AZTECS HAD VERY DEFINITE IDEAS ABOUT SOCIAL classes. The three social classes—nobility, commoner, and slave—were clearly defined and strictly maintained. The nobility or the upper class of Aztec society was the *pipiltin*. The commoners were part of the *macehualli*. People were born into their class, and few ever rose above it.

The social rules for professions were even more rigid. Children of goldsmiths became goldsmiths, farmers' children were farmers, scribes' sons were scribes, and so on.

Although the majority of people had no choice about their lifestyle or career, some highly gifted children did rise above their parents' status. Young men all trained for the military. A skilled warrior could earn wealth by his brave deeds and could also rise in social status—although the chances for this rise were slim. Another opportunity for success came through talent. Skilled weavers, outstanding singers, and very smart boys could also advance. Boys who showed promise in the *macehualli* school could be sent to the *calmecac*, a school for nobles.

Another way to rise above low status was to be promised to the priesthood. Parents could commit their children, boys or girls, to the temple at birth. One reason to commit a child to the priesthood was the improved standard of living. Children in the temple were fed, housed, and clothed. They did not need to fear dying of hunger in times of famine.

PIPILTIN, THE NOBILITY

The Aztec noble class began with Acamapichtli, the first *tlatoani*. He had several wives and many children. He created a ruling dynasty. The

OPPOSITE

Aztec soldiers dressed in magnificent uniforms. Eagle warriors, as represented by this statue, were one of the two specially honored classes of Aztec soldiers.

How Is It Pronounced?

Calmecac
kahl-MeH-kahk

Calpixqui
kahl-PEESH-kee

Calpulli
kahl-POO-lee

Chinampas
chee-NAHM-pahs

Macehualli
mah-seh-WALL-ee

Pipiltin
pee-PEEL-teen

Pochteca
pohch-TAY-kuh

closer a person was connected to his family through marriage or blood, the more prestige they had.

Nobles gained status through good marriages to others with wealth or power, military success, or service to the empire. Members of this group filled high positions in the government, owned private land, and gained other advantages. By the mid 1300s, the noble class had become an established social group, the *pipiltin*. People were born into the nobility or rose to noble status by acts of military heroism. Noble status was hereditary—it was inherited from parents to children, and never lost. If nobles married commoners, their children were also part of the nobility.

Despite their privilege, nobles were not expected or allowed to be lazy. Even the highest noble was expected to work, achieve, lead in the military, and make sacrifices. The Aztecs would not support a group of rich people who did no work and lived only for pleasure.

Still, there were some obvious advantages to being a noble. The *pipiltin* lived well and ate well. Many had estates with grand, two-story houses—an honor not allowed commoners. They ate meat and fish, vegetables, fruits, and had the best foods available. Nobles were allowed to wear gold jewelry and cotton clothing, and they usually wore bright colors. Motecuhzoma II made it illegal for commoners to wear cotton, and anyone who defied that law suffered the death penalty.

Being noble also brought responsibilities. The extent of these responsibilities was drilled into the minds of the young at school. Noble girls and boys attended the *calmecac,* which was attached to the temple. Girls and boys attended separate schools. Under the guidance of the priest-schoolmaster, children learned to pray, fast, and sacrifice. They were taught to suffer pain by cutting themselves as part of blood sacrifices. They also learned Aztec history and customs by reading codices. The boys trained to be warriors, which was an obligation of all male Aztecs.

All noble men had jobs. They were expected to run their estates and also have another position. Many became government administrators and managed such tasks as tax collecting, road building, temple building, or farming. In addition to these jobs, they might also be asked to serve as judges or military leaders. Others became priests in one of the many Aztec temples.

Noble women were expected to oversee the workings of their home. This could be a big job. A noble woman was expected to attend to the same chores as a commoner wife, although she might have many servants to do the actual work. Still, she had to make sure all family members, slaves, and workers were fed, housed, and clothed. The cleaning of the home, the health of its members, and the early education of the children were also her responsibility.

THE *TLATOANI*

Every *altepetl* (city-state, although some were quite rural) had a *tlatoani*. Each was like a king. After the Aztecs defeated the Tepanec and began their military expansion, the *tlatoani* of Tenochtitlan ruled as an emperor. He was the most powerful and feared of all Aztecs.

The *tlatoani* was the commander-in-chief of the military and the high priest of the religion. Every decision he made influenced the people of the empire. If he called for higher taxes, the people had to pay. He could condemn a person to death, take away wealth, or declare war. During a famine, the *tlatoani* could open the royal granaries and feed the people—or order more human sacrifices to please the gods.

The *tlatoani* always came from the Aztec royal family, which was extensive. There were many brothers and sisters, children, cousins, aunts and uncles, and husbands and wives. *Tlatoque* were allowed to have up to 100 wives, so they usually had plenty of children.

To choose the *tlatoani*, a council of elders—all nobles—picked from among four candidates. All were usually close relatives of the previous *tlatoani*. These candidates were young men who showed the most intelligence, the greatest wit, and the most courage in battle. Aztec *tlatoque* did not automatically pass their office on to their sons. However, in some city-states this was the practice. For example, in Texcoco Nezahualcoyotl was followed by his son, Nezahualpilli, who passed his office on to his son, Cacamac.

Once chosen, the *tlatoani* of Tenochtitlan was *tlatoani* for life. When he took office, the Aztecs held a huge coronation ceremony. The new *tlatoani* went to the top of a temple to hear lectures by the elders. The lectures were called the *huehuetlatolli*, or "speeches of the elders." The *tlatoani* learned what his new job required and the tremendous responsibility he was taking on. All Aztecs depended on him.

A massive feast and the presentation of gifts followed the lectures. Every noble guest gave the *tlatoani* a present. He looked on at the feast and the entertainment from a throne decorated with feathers, and he

Lords of the Aztecs

While the *tlatoani* was the supreme power within a city-state, he sometimes gave land to a class of nobles called *tetecuhtin* (the singular was a *tecuhilt*). These "lords," as they are sometimes called in English, could pass their lands on to their descendants when they died. Like a *tlatoani*, the *tetecuhtin* received tribute. This came from the commoners who worked the lords' lands. Some nobles below the *tetecuhtin* in social rank owed loyalty to them, and might live near a *tecuhitl's* palace so they could provide service to their lord.

wore a fine robe and a magnificent crown. From then on, he led a life of great luxury and much greater responsibility.

AZTEC PRIESTS

After the *tlatoani*, the most powerful positions in Aztec society were held by the high priests. There were two high priests and many ranks of priests below them, similar to ranks of military leaders. It was the main job of the priests to keep the gods happy and let the people know what they needed to do to make the gods content.

The highest ranks of priests belonged to the noble class, the *pipiltin*. Other priests could come from any social class, and many children were promised to serve in the priesthood.

Priests performed many roles in the temple. Some supervised the business of the temple, while others prepared for and performed sacrifices. Some priests were destined to be teachers and taught boys in the *calmecac*. The most powerful priests worked in the Great Temple that served the sun god and the god of rain. Priests could also belong to the military. They marched to war beside their fellow soldiers.

Lower ranked priests, usually from commoner families, served the higher priests. They dressed all in black. Some also painted their bodies black while others wore long black cloaks with hoods.

Women could become priestesses. This was an excellent life for women who did not marry. Priestesses served the many goddesses the Aztecs worshipped. Like priests, the priestesses had many jobs within their temples. Some also took on the role of their goddess in parades and festivals. Certain priestesses took part in human sacrifices to goddesses, while others gave followers gifts of maize or other foods.

WARRIORS

War was a way of life for the Aztecs. Warriors went to war with great joy. Courage, strength, and fearlessness in the face of the enemy were qualities much admired in the Aztec culture.

Warriors began their training as children. The Aztec military had no permanent soldiers, but it did have a full range of professional officers. The leading commander was the *tlatoani*, which is one reason why bravery in combat was a qualification for becoming the *tlatoani*.

Priestly Hair

Spanish Priest Bernal Díaz del Castillo wrote about the hair of the Aztec priests he saw: "They wore their hair very long, down to the waist, with some even reaching down to the feet" (quoted in *The Discovery and Conquest of Mexico*). As soon as boys began studying for the priesthood, they began growing their hair long. Adult priests never cut their hair. They tied it back with a white ribbon and covered it with soot. Díaz noted that after a sacrifice, the priest's hair was covered with blood.

Every healthy man age 17 and up was expected to fight whenever he was called upon.

Soldiers dressed in magnificent uniforms. There were two honored groups—jaguar knights and eagle knights. Members of those troops wore special helmets and carried special shields. A jaguar warrior might wear a uniform made of animal skins, while an eagle warrior had a helmet shaped like the sharp beak of an eagle. They also wore their hair in distinctive styles that drew attention to their rank and their heroic acts on the battlefield. The greater the feats displayed, the more elaborately a warrior dressed and decorated himself.

A warrior had to be skilled in the use of several weapons: spears, slings, bows and arrows, darts and dart-throwers, knives, and swords. The blades of weapons were made from sharpened obsidian, which was very sharp but easily broken.

Historian Miguel Léon-Portilla (b. 1926), an authority on the Aztecs, wrote (in *The Broken Spears: The Aztec Account of the Conquest of Mexico*), "A war or battle always commenced with a certain ritual: shields, arrows, and cloaks of a special kind were sent to the enemy leaders as a formal declaration that they would soon be attacked. This explains the Aztecs' surprise when the Spaniards, their

A Priestess's Life

Young girls might be dedicated to the temple as children, even if they would not become priestesses. Such girls usually lived in the temples and learned specific jobs within the temple grounds. Most priestesses did not usually carry out religious rites. They were "housewives" of the temple, cleaning, gardening, and cooking for the gods and the priests who served them.

CONNECTIONS

The Jaguar and the Ocelot

The jaguar was a very important animal to the Aztecs. It is the largest wildcat in the Americas and is a fierce hunter. Because jaguars see well at night, the Aztecs associated them with Tezcatlipoca, the god of night.

The Aztecs chose the jaguar as a symbol for some of their best warriors because of the big cat's bravery. Their word for the jaguar was *ocelotl*. Today, that word is the root of the name of another wildcat, a smaller relative of the jaguar called the ocelot.

An ocelot is twice the size of the average housecat and has a spotted coat. Many ocelots live in the rain forests of Central and South America. But they can also be found as far north as Texas. Ocelots are currently endangered.

guests, suddenly turned on them without any apparent motive and—more important—without the customary ritual warning."

The goal of war was not to kill the enemy but to expand territory and collect captives. Warriors struck the enemy in the legs with a sword. Success for a warrior was based on the number of captives taken. This was sometimes a way for a commoner to gain a promotion in rank and possibly even become a noble.

In the 11th month of each year, the *tlatoani* gave out military honors and awards. These might include special weapons and badges of distinction, shields, swords, cloaks, and loincloths.

The army was divided into small groups of about 200 men that were like modern platoons. The basic large unit, like today's battalion, had about 8,000 men. A major war would see as many as 25 units, or 200,000 warriors, heading to battle.

Along with the warriors were porters to carry supplies. Before a war began, communities were warned in advance. Each *calpulli* was expected to provide 400 warriors, along with supplies. Towns had their orders to provide quantities of maize, tortillas, salt, beans, fresh and dried chilies, corn meal, and pumpkin seeds to feed the troops.

MACEHUALLI, THE COMMONERS

Commoners had a wide range of jobs. They were merchants, traders, artisans, craftsmen, and farmers. Merchants and traders provided the

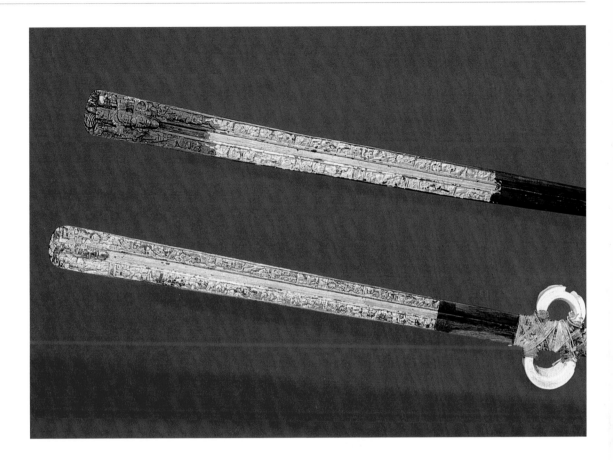

goods available in the markets. Traders traveled far and wide to collect the products that were sold. Because the Aztecs had no wagons or other vehicles to carry their goods, traders moved their goods by canoe if there were waterways, or they had slaves called porters carry their products on their backs.

Traders, called *pochteca* (the singular is *pochtecatl*), traveled on foot to distant nations. They traded for luxury items, such as brilliantly colored feathers, gems, and animal hides. Some *pochteca* also traded in slaves. The travel was dangerous, and some traders wisely took warriors with them along with the porters needed to carry their goods. Smart *pochteca* never wore fancy clothing or announced their wealth. They traveled in plain clothing and often at night so they did not attract the attention of robbers. Some traders traveled in groups for safety.

Farmers grew their own food and paid tribute in the form of crops. They could also sell any extra crops in the marketplace. Farmers who

An Aztec warrior had to be skilled in using a spear. These are *atlatl*, or spear throwers. They are made of gold and covered with designs showing gods and warriors. Gold items were made for show and ceremony, and were not taken into an actual battle.

This panel from a larger work made of deerskin shows Yacatecuhtli, the god of merchants, at the upper left and scenes of merchants in the other squares.

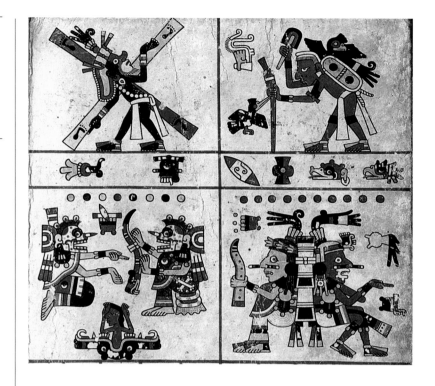

did not have access to a local market to sell their extra food traded with a traveling *pochtecatl*.

SLAVES

The lowest social class consisted of slaves. People could become slaves as punishment for committing crimes. Stealing and selling stolen goods were punished by slavery. So was kidnapping children with the idea of selling the children as slaves. Some cities were required to provide a specific number of slaves each year as part of their tribute. They went hunting for those slaves from cultures beyond the Aztec Empire.

Some slaves were former enemies who had been captured during a war. Most captured men would consider slavery far better than the other alternative they faced—sacrifice. Prisoners of war could only become slaves or sacrifices.

Most people volunteered to enter slavery. To the Aztecs, free people were entitled to live their lives as they saw fit. If they chose to sell themselves into slavery, that was fine. By doing so, they would always have food, clothing, and shelter.

Finally, some people became slaves through debt. A family might enter into a business arrangement with someone who was wealthy. The parents could sell one of their sons to the official or noble in return for land, food, or a home. This was a common practice when food was in short supply. During such a crisis, it was better to sell a child into slavery than to watch that child starve to death.

The life of an Aztec slave was not as difficult as it has been for slaves in other cultures and at other times. Aztec slaves were always fed, housed, and clothed, and male slaves did not have to serve in the military. Since the Aztecs went to war regularly, military service was dangerous. Slaves did not have to pay taxes. This was a real advantage in a society that taxed everything.

On the other hand, slaves were not considered citizens. They were property, like any other object. Slaves worked for a master, usually a man. They might do farm work, serve in a household, or be a porter

Tlatelolco Market

The largest market was in Tlatelolco. A shopper could find everything from lengths of rough cloth to golden necklaces, simple clay pots to ornately carved wooden chests, and corn to exotic foods such as spirulina—a type of algae from the surface of ponds—and beetles.

In addition to traders, the marketplace was also a place for artisans and craftspeople to sell the goods they made. This was the place where skilled weavers or dyers offered their goods for sale. The Aztecs had many skilled craftspeople, including leather workers, stone workers, brick makers, gold and silversmiths, feather artists, and potters.

The market offered services, as well. Customers could get a haircut, hire a porter who would carry items for them, or grab a bite to eat in a café. The merchants and craftspeople, however, were the main focus, and they had to follow strict rules.

At the Tlatelolco market, each business day began and ended with the beating of a drum. All the sellers of a particular item were restricted to certain areas of the market. Everyone had to use the same standard measurements for selling items by length or volume. The merchants also could not change the prices of goods, because these were set in advance. If government officials caught merchants trying to cheat a buyer, the merchants were punished.

Slave Traders

Slave traders were among the most respected *pochteca* in Aztec society. They were called *tlaltlanime*, which means "washers of slaves." This name refers to the fact that slaves had to be bathed before they were sacrificed. The slave traders were the wealthiest of all traders. They were honored because some of the slaves they provided played such an important role in religious ceremonies.

for a trader. Female slaves spun thread, wove cloth, mended clothes, and cooked food. These were the same tasks expected of a commoner's wife.

Several things made Aztec slavery different from slavery in some other cultures. Slaves could learn and work in skilled trades, and many slaves held positions of importance in a household. A slave could be a scribe, who wrote official documents, or an accountant, who kept financial records. Slaves were allowed to own property, buy and sell goods, and save money.

Slaves were allowed to marry and raise children. They could marry other slaves, or they could marry free men or women. Marriage to a slave did not mean giving up one's freedom, and slaves could eventually become free. Children born of slaves were not slaves. They were considered free, and being the child of a slave was not embarrassing. In fact, the great *tlatoani* Itzcoatl had a mother who was a slave.

Generally, new slaves were traded in a slave market. The slaves were brought to market with wooden collars around their necks. They were tied to a long pole to prevent escape. While it was easy to buy new slaves, slave owners could not easily sell any of their current slaves. The law allowed the sale only of slaves who were violent or lazy. Such a slave could be bought and sold for work three times. After that, the next purchase usually was for the festival of Panquetzaliztli, held at harvest time—this festival required the sacrifice of slaves. No one wanted to sacrifice a hard-working, valuable slave. Instead, many bought lazy slaves specifically for the sacrifice.

The buying and selling of slaves was a bustling, profitable business. An average slave cost about 20 cotton cloaks. A talented or skilled slave, such as a singer or a scribe, might cost as much as 40 cotton cloaks. Two commoners could live for an entire year on what it would cost to buy a singer or a scribe.

Most slaves were not Aztec. They were brought to the empire as captives. However, all slaves had an opportunity to gain freedom. A slave who was being sold in the market could try running away when he or she was put up for sale. If the slave reached the ruler's palace before being caught by his or her owner or the owner's son, the slave became free. No one else in the city was allowed to help the slave-holder by stopping the runaway slave. To interfere in the chase was a crime, and the person who committed this crime was punished by being made a slave.

THE *CALPULLI*

In Aztec society, every person regardless of social status belonged to a *calpulli*. As the people moved into the cities, *calpulli* evolved into districts or neighborhoods. Each *calpulli* had its own leader, council, temple, and schools. Each had its own *calpulli* council and was responsible for choosing council leaders to keep the district running smoothly. The districts were political divisions, much like voting districts in today's counties, cities, or towns. When the Spanish arrived in Tenochtitlan, the city had 80 *calpulli*.

In rural areas, the *calpulli* owned land as a group. The farmers worked the land together and used water owned by the *calpulli* members. The *calpulli* paid tribute as a group, and everyone worked to ensure an excellent harvest. That harvest paid the tribute, fed the people, and provided surplus crops that the *calpulli members* could trade at the market.

HOW THE AZTECS EARNED A LIVING

In Aztec culture, every healthy person was expected to work. Children learned when they were toddlers that they would have to work to live. The economy was based on farming, so most people earned their living by growing food. The main crop was maize or corn, the staple food of the Aztec diet.

The people who lived in cities had more luxuries than those in farm districts. The people of Tenochtitlan needed an active, vital economy to support their larger homes and their higher social status. At the height of the Aztec Empire, the city's population varied from 100,000 to 300,000 people. Those people needed food, services, arts, and goods. The city supported farming, crafts, and an active religious life.

Farming was the heart of the Aztec economy. The people needed food and clothing, and farming provided both. The Aztecs had only hand tools to help them farm, and they had no large animals to assist them, such as horses, mules, or oxen. The Aztecs grew a wide range of vegetables, including avocados, beans, chilies, squash, tomatoes, and onions. For grain, they grew maize and amaranth. Farmers also raised turkeys and dogs for meat.

The land the Aztecs farmed was not fertile enough to grow all the food needed to support the population. So the Aztecs needed to find a way to produce more food. They found ways to irrigate, or bring water

Valuable Cotton

Cotton cloth was highly valued. But it could not be grown in the Valley of Mexico because it is too cool there. Cotton was imported from lower, warmer territories to the south, in today's state of Morelos in Mexico. Cotton came into the Aztec Empire as trade or tribute. In fact, the desire for cotton was a motivation for the Aztecs' first conquests.

CONNECTIONS

Building *Chinampas*

The process of making *chinampas* was simple. First, canals were cut through the marshes and swamps. The farmer then marked out a square plot, using mud and plants to form walls to hold back the water. Mud was then placed on mats made from reeds, which lined the bottom of the plot.

Willow trees were planted along the walls of the plot. When the trees took root, they acted like anchors that kept the walls of the *chinampas* in place. At that point, the *chinampa* could be used for planting maize.

The use of *chinampas* did not die out with the end of the Aztec Empire. They are still used today in a region southeast of Mexico City, particularly near a lake called Xochimilco. Farmers grow maize, flowers, and vegetables on their island farms.

The gardens of Xochimilco are all that remain of the Aztec island farms known as *chinampas*.

from its source to their farms. They also used fertilizers (chemicals that help crops grow). The Aztecs also built raised platforms of soil, called terraces, to grow food on hillsides. Their most original idea, however, was their island farms, *chinampas*.

Planting, weeding, and harvesting maize on a *chinampa* was hard work. Everyone in a farming family took part in the work. Once the corn was harvested, each ear of maize had to be shucked (the outer husk pulled off) and the kernels removed from the cob. The corn was then dried and stored. Although the corn could be used as dried kernels, it was normally made into a dough, which was used to make porridge or tortillas. Farmers often paid their taxes in the form of fresh or dried corn.

Extra food could be traded in the town market. Cloth, leather, wooden items, and any other crafts could also be traded in the marketplace. The Aztecs had no coins or paper money, but they did use cacao beans as a form or currency.

Cacao beans were precious to the Aztecs, who used them to make chocolate. The beans were small and portable. A person could easily carry a pouch with several hundred cacao beans and use them to buy goods or services anywhere in the Aztec Empire. Cacao beans were often used in local markets to buy tools, clothes, leather for sandals, and jewelry. Gold, silver, and precious stones were expensive and cost plenty of beans.

The two largest markets were in Tenochtitlan and Tlatelolco. These were held outdoors in specific market areas. Market day was a celebration of food, crafts, and color. People from every *calpulli* and from neighboring towns went to these markets to buy or trade goods. This was a place where a farmer could trade avocados for a length of rope or tomatoes for an axe head. There was cloth, leather, jewelry, pottery, carvings of stone and wood—any item an Aztec farmer or craftsmen produced was for sale.

The market was a place for socializing, too. The market at Tlatelolco often had a crowd as large as 25,000. The sellers, often professional market women, laid out their goods on mats on the ground. Shoppers moved from vendor to vendor, looking for the food or goods they needed.

GOVERNMENT OFFICIALS

The *tlatoani* was the head of the Aztec government. As the empire grew, the *tlatoani* needed more people to make the government function. These officials were chosen by the *tlatoani* and reported directly to him.

Officials were public servants, much as governors, mayors, generals, and senators are today. The Aztecs expected such officials to meet high standards. They had to be loyal, honest, and morally superior. Any public official who was dishonest was punished.

Historian Jacques Soustelle writes (in *Daily Life of the Aztecs*), "[T]he laws and customs were terribly severe: woe to the drunken judge, the over accommodating judge; woe to the dishonest civil servant. The sentence of the king of Texcoco was always quoted as an example—he, hearing that one of his judges had favoured a noble against a *macehualli,* had the unrighteous justice hanged. If the power was very great, the duties were very heavy."

Being a government official offered great rewards but made even greater demands. Usually, high officials were landowners who often had property in several areas. They spent much of their time traveling between estates. In the meantime, the work of the estate had to be done. Trusted stewards, or top aides, made sure an estate was productive while the owner worked as an officer of the courts, judge, tax collector, or military leader. The owner might also be an ambassador to another city-state or a schoolteacher. The demands of public service were heavy, particularly for a judge, who might have to oversee the execution of a convicted criminal or sit in a court session that lasted up to 10 or 12 hours.

The primary jobs of a government official were overseeing the planting and harvests, and collecting taxes and tribute. The main tax collector was the *calpixqui*, who might have been little more than a trained servant. The *calpixque* (plural form) reviewed the economy and agriculture of the district for which they were responsible.

Calpixque lived in the main town or district that they looked after. They kept track of how productive agriculture was, noting problems such as drought or insects. The *calpixque* also noted any trade with outside groups and any increased income or surpluses in products produced in the town. If the area needed a new public building, better roads, or slaves to care for public facilities, a *calpixqui* was responsible for making sure these things happened. If there was a famine, a *calpixqui* sent a message to the *tlatoani*. In turn, the *tlatoani* might say the town did not have to pay tribute that season or the town could draw on the *tlatoani's* stores of dried maize for food.

The *calpixqui* hired scribes to keep up with the amount of work involved in their jobs. Scribes kept records of the current events in the town, the taxes owed and paid, and other public activities.

AZTEC LAWS

Motecuhzoma Ilhuicamina is often credited with making sure the Aztec legal system was honest and fair. The Aztecs certainly had a collection of laws before Motecuhzoma became *tlatoani*. But he did introduce new rules that made sure the laws would be applied in the same way for everyone.

Trials could be held throughout the empire. A jury heard the evidence against the accused person. The jury consisted of a head judge, who ran the trial, and several other judges as well. They listened to witnesses who saw the crime or looked at other evidence. If the criminal was an important person or a noble, the trial might be heard by the *tlatoani*.

The jury decided whether a person was guilty. The head judge then passed sentence on anyone found guilty. Guilty people knew that there was no room for mercy. The sentences were already set out in the legal code.

Anyone tried and convicted in a lower court could appeal the verdict to a council, much like today's supreme court. The *tlatoani* appointed judges to this council.

The *tlatoani* was not only the Aztecs' government leader, he was also the head judge. The laws were very simple, and the punishments were severe. People learned from an early age that they had to obey the law. The Aztecs wanted order in their society, and they got it.

The Aztecs had the same types of crimes that society has today. However, not all criminals were treated equally. Aztec nobles who committed crimes generally received harsher sentences than commoners. They lived a life of privilege and were expected to know better than to commit a crime. Thus, they deserved greater punishment if they were found guilty.

IN THEIR OWN WORDS

Order in the Court

Most judges were nobles, although some were chosen by the *tlatoani* from among commoners who were well brought up and were good warriors. Spanish priest and historian Bernadino de Sahagún noted some of the qualities the ruler looked for in good judges.

> Such as these the ruler gave office and chose as his judges—the wise, the able, the sage; who listened and spoke well; who were of good memory; who spoke not vainly or lightly; who did not make friends without forethought nor were drunkards; who guarded their lineage with honor; who slept not overmuch, [but rather] arose early; who did nothing for friendship's or kinship's sake, nor for enmity; who would not hear or judge a case for a fee. The ruler might condemn them to death; hence they performed their offices as judges righteously.

The last sentence explains that if a judge unfairly favored one person, such as a friend or relative, or took a bribe, he could be executed.

(Source: Sahagún, Bernardino de, General. *History of the Things of New Spain (Florentine Codex).* vol. 8. Translated by Charles E. Dibble and Arthur J.O. Anderson. Reprint. Santa Fe, N.M.: School of American Research and the University of Utah Press, 1979.)

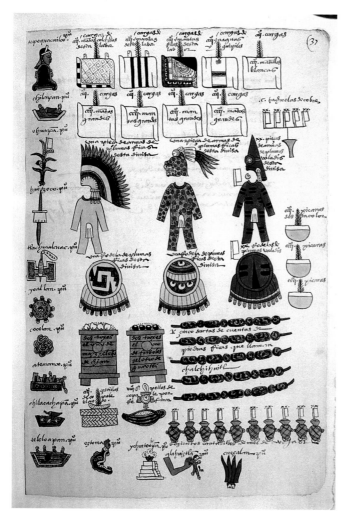

This page from the Codex Mendoza shows the tribute paid to Aztec rulers by people living in the empire.

Treason—disloyalty to the government—was the worst of crimes. A traitor was put to death, the family lost all its property, and the children were sold into slavery. The sentence for anyone convicted of murder, adultery (cheating on a spouse), or major theft was death. This was also true for people caught moving a field boundary marker. These markers showed who owned what land, so moving one amounted to stealing land.

People who were drunk in public had their heads shaved and their houses destroyed. For a second offense, the drunken person was put to death. Any commoner found wearing cotton clothing was put to death. Cutting down a living tree also brought the death penalty. Death sentences were usually carried out by stoning, beating, or strangling the guilty person.

People who committed lesser crimes were expected to make good on what they had done. For example, a thief had to return stolen goods. Several crimes earned a sentence of slavery. Handling stolen property, kidnapping, and minor theft meant a criminal would be sold as a slave. Anyone in the marketplace caught selling poor quality goods lost their property. The penalty for committing slander—speaking falsely about someone—was having one's lips cut off. With such severe penalties for crimes, the Aztecs were a very law-abiding people.

PAYING TAXES AND TRIBUTE

Everyone in the Aztec Empire paid tax and tribute, except for the *tlatoani*, high officials, priests, children, orphans, and slaves. Commoners paid with their work. Artists and craftsmen paid with goods. Towns, cities, and conquered nations paid with crops, cotton, animals, precious metals, paper—anything that had value.

Government officials were charged with determining how much was owed from each province and recording the payment. Tribute was paid on a regular schedule, usually once or twice a year.

The majority of the tribute went to supporting the *tlatoani* and his vast household. The tribute was not spread evenly among the people living in the empire. The *tlatoani*, nobles, and priests got the majority of the taxes paid. The commoners, merchants, and traders paid the taxes.

Each town paid taxes based on it particular situation. Some were required to maintain the *tlatoani's* palaces, while others were expected to feed the royal household. The *Codex Mendoza* records the annual fees paid by seven towns as "4,000 mantles and loincloths, 800 bales of dried chilies, 20 bags of down feathers, two war-dresses and shields, three strings of precious stones, and two plates inlaid with turquoise" (quoted in *Law in Mexico Before the Conquest*).

IN THEIR OWN WORDS

Payment in Insects

Spanish priest Diego Durán noted some of the more unusual forms of tribute the Aztec rulers collected from their subjects.

These nations paid tribute to the Mexicans with live birds, the most precious with rich plumage; some green, other red or blue; parrots, big and small, and all kinds of elegant colored birds, eagles, eagle-owls, sparrow-hawks, kestrels, crows, herons, geese, big goslings.

There were wild animals of all kinds; tribute was paid with live lions and tigers, and wild cats; all kids of wild animals, they were brought in cages. Then snakes, big and small poisonous and non-venomous, wild and tame. . . . Even centipedes, scorpions, spider, they asked for them in tribute, thus making themselves lords of every creature; everything was theirs and belonged to them!

(Source: Durán, Diego. *The History of the Indies of New Spain.* Translated by Doris Heyden. Norman, Okla.: University of Oklahoma Press, 1994.)

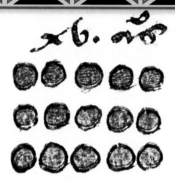

xb.

Fogon

muger   baron

sahumerio

estera

comida   comida

CHAPTER 5

DAILY LIFE AMONG THE AZTECS

THE BASIC UNIT OF AZTEC LIFE WAS THE HOUSEHOLD. Households were usually comprised of people who were related. A household could be just a mother and father and their children, or two related families, or a family plus aunts, uncles, and grandparents..

In fact, there is no Nahuatl word for "family." The closest thing is *cemithualtin*, which means "those of one courtyard." In a city, the family group might all live in one large house or in a cluster of houses connected to one another.

Political power was mostly in the hands of men. At home, the father was the head of the family, but the mother was nearly equal in many ways. Both had very specific roles to play in making sure the family had what it needed. The women did not do men's work and the men did not do women's work, but both were seen as equally important to the functioning of society and, in fact, the entire world.

Women depended on men to grow corn, but men were just as dependent on women to process it into tortillas and other foods. Men won glory through battle, but often women were the healers who tended to them when they came home wounded. Women were supreme in certain important household areas, such as making cloth.

The high priests of the Aztec religion were all men, but at home, women maintained the sacred hearth fire, swept (which maintained the ritual purity of the home), made daily offerings to the fire and household gods, and performed rituals when their husbands were away at war that would help ensure their success in battle. In some cases, particularly with craftsmen, wives also helped their husbands with their jobs.

OPPOSITE
This illustration shows a typical Aztec marriage ceremony. Marriage was an important ritual for the Aztecs, and all marriages were arranged by the families of the bride and groom.

How Is It Pronounced?

Cuicacalli
    kwee-kah-KAH-lee
Macehualtin
    mah-say-HWAHL-teen
Telpochcalli
    tell-pohch-KAH-lee

Both mothers and fathers played a role in raising and educating children. Mothers raised the youngest boys and girls. As a boy grew older, his father took charge of teaching him the skills he would need as an adult. Boys usually followed in their father's trade. Fathers also taught sons how to farm and fish. As girls grew up, they learned from their mothers the household duties they would perform. These included the key tasks of making offerings and carrying out household religious rituals.

HOME SWEET HOME

Throughout history, people usually built their homes using whatever local materials were most plentiful. For the Aztecs, this was adobe bricks. Brick makers used the water, clay, and reeds of their land to form building blocks. Adobe bricks were dried in the sun and were strong and solid. But they could fall apart in heavy rains.

Most houses were small, one-room structures. The doorways were square, the roofs flat, and the walls thick. One advantage of a flat roof was that it provided added sleeping space on hot nights.

Nobles and wealthy merchants might have two-story homes made of stone. These homes had gardens, pools, and a central courtyard for shade. Wealthy families could afford larger homes, and the highest nobles lived in palaces.

Even humble homes had all the basics a family needed. All houses had hearths on which to cook, although large homes had actual kitchens. There was always a place to wash, a place for sleeping, and a shrine for family religious rites.

Homes did not have a lot of furniture. Both the rich and the

Strict Parents

With both girls and boys, parents used strict punishments to make sure the children learned their tasks well and took them seriously. Even when their children were young, parents punished them for laziness or disobedience.

At around 8 years old, children might be stuck with cactus spines on their hands as a punishment. Parents might also pinch their arms or ears. When they were older, the children could be beaten with sticks as punishment for poor performance. The worst children faced was parents who made them breathe in the smoke of roasting chili peppers.

The lines at the bottom of these Aztec pots suggest that they were used for grinding pepper.

poor slept on reed mats called *petlatl*. The quality and comfort of the mats the rich owned may have been better than the mats owned by peasants, but they were basically alike. The mats and blankets were placed on a platform called *tlapechtli*, which served as a bed. In poorer homes, bed mats also provided seating in the daytime.

The highest nobles sat on low chairs made of wicker. Some had cushions, and many had raised backs against which the sitter could lean and rest. Only the *tlatoani* and the highest nobles had what might be considered fine furniture. This furniture followed the same basic design as other Aztec furniture, but it was covered with embroidered cloth or skins of jaguars or other animals instead of reed mats.

The Aztecs stored blankets, household goods, and clothing in chests. Most people had wicker or reed chests and baskets for storage. Only the wealthy had wooden chests. Food was stored in pottery jars. Every kitchen, no matter how crude, had a bowl and a grinding stone for making dried corn into dough.

Riches in the Garbage

The Aztecs kept their homes very clean. In rural areas, garbage from the home was thrown into heaps next to or behind the building. These piles are called *middens*, and the remains of them are sometimes uncovered today. Middens are important finds for archaeologists. By studying the items people threw away—such as the remains of broken clay pots and plates, tools used for spinning, and small religious objects— the archaeologists learn more about Aztec life.

Unwanted House Guests

The Aztecs believed ants, frogs, and mice brought bad luck. People thought a swarm of ants in a house was a curse on the homeowners—perhaps an enemy planted something evil in the floor of a person's home. That evil thing erupted into a swarm of ants. Since the Aztecs slept and ate on floor mats, a swarm of ants could be particularly unpleasant.

Frogs and toads were common enough in Aztec times. The only ones that brought bad luck were those that ended up in a person's home. The croaking drove people mad!

Finally, there was the mouse, a common thief who ate grain and other foods, leaving homeowners hungry. The Aztecs believed that if a person ate maize that had been nibbled by mice, that person would become like the mouse—a thief who sneaks into the homes of others and steals from them.

FOOD AND DRINK

The foods the Aztecs loved the most are available in any Mexican restaurant today. They are the foods of the Americas: corn, beans, squash, tomatoes, peppers, and avocados.

The staple grain was corn, or maize. From childhood, girls learned how to make tortillas—flat bread made from corn meal. The Aztecs ate tortillas every day. They were served filled with beans, vegetables, or meats. Farmers took tortillas into the field for their afternoon meal.

Tamalli (today's tamales) was maize dough filled with chilies, beans, or meat and formed into a ball. The dough was then steamed in a clay pot, much like a dumpling. *Atolli* was maize porridge to which fruit or chilies were added for flavor. *Pozolli*, a soup with whole corn kernels, was filling and nutritious. Today it is known as *pozole* in Spanish.

The Aztecs raised only two domestic animals for meat: dogs and turkeys. They did not have cattle, pigs, or sheep until after the arrival of the Spanish. Meat was expensive, and the protein source for most people was beans, which were eaten daily. Hunters added to the average diet by providing deer, rabbit, ducks, geese, and other birds. Grasshoppers and agave worms were roasted and eaten, along with other kinds of protein-rich insects and larvae.

Grains, vegetables, and fruits made up most of the Aztec diet. In addition to maize-based foods, tomatoes and chilies were common. The tomatoes were distant relatives of today's tomatoes. There were smaller and fewer varieties were available. Chili peppers provided a full range of hotness, from very mild to mouth-searing hot. The Aztecs also ate onions, sweet potatoes, jicama, peanuts, and popcorn.

The chip-and-dip dish called guacamole today was actually a sauce in Aztec times. It is made with avocados, tomatoes, and onions. It was added to a dish fit only for the *tlatoani* and his guests—roasted agave worms. The Aztecs used salt and chili peppers to season their

IN THEIR OWN WORDS

Rich Food, Poor Food

A meal in Aztec times varied, depending on the wealth of the person eating and the occasion. Spanish priest and historian Bernal Díaz del Castillo described in his journal one of Motecuhzoma II's dinners. (A brazier is a small device used to hold coals when cooking food.)

> His cooks prepared over 30 kinds of dishes for every meal, done the way he liked them; and they placed small pottery braziers under them so they wouldn't get cold. They prepared over three hundred plates of the food Montezuma was going to eat, and more than a thousand plates for the guard. . . . Every day they cooked chicken, turkey, pheasant, partridge, quail, tame and wild duck, venison, wild pig . . . hares, rabbits, and many varieties of birds and other things that grow in this country. . . .

In contrast to this daily banquet for the *tlatoani*, Bernardino de Sahagún described the poor choices offered at a feast thrown by a commoner.

> But among those who were only commoners . . . only miserably, in poverty and want, were receptions and invitations made. Not as much was offered one as was required and customary. . . . Many things were omitted or spoiled. Thus [the feast] was a failure and fruitless . . . perhaps only leftovers, bitter sauces, and stale tamales and tortillas were offered them.

(Source: Díaz del Castillo, Bernal. *The Bernal Díaz Chronicle.* Translated and edited by Albert Idell. Garden City, N.Y.: Dolphin Books, 1956; and *General History of the Things of New Spain (Florentine Codex).* Vol. 4. Translated by Charles E. Dibble and Arthur J. O. Anderson. Reprint. Santa Fe, N.M.: School of American Research and the University of Utah Press, 1979.)

Only the richest Aztec households would serve cocoa, often in fancy vessels such as this one shaped like a hare.

food. They also used a flavoring popular today: vanilla. Vanilla comes from the seed pod of a variety of orchid. It is still found in Mexican dishes. For those who could afford it, a meal was finished with a cup of chocolate.

The major alcoholic beverage of the Aztecs was *octli*. Brewers collected sap from the agave plant. The sap would be boiled and fermented until it was as smooth as honey. The drink was loaded with vitamins and had less alcohol than today's beer. People still sometimes drank enough to get drunk, though. The Aztecs had many rules meant to keep people from drinking too much, but they were not always followed.

CONNECTIONS

Ancient Treats

Popcorn and chewing gum are popular treats in the United States, and both have roots in Mesoamerican culture. The average American chewed 300 sticks (or chiclets or lumps) of gum a year. While the Aztecs did not have watermelon-, grape-, or mint-flavored varieties, they did chew gum. They chewed chicle (the natural gum of a tropical evergreen tree), bitumen, and other gums and saps to clean their teeth.

The oldest ears of corn ever used to make popcorn were found in the Bat Cave in central Mexico. The scientists who found this popcorn in 1948 saw kernels much like those popped today. In fact, they took a handful of the kernels and popped them in hot oil. Poof! Antique popcorn!

How old was that corn? It was tested and found to be 5,600 years old. Historians believe that early people popped the corn by placing it on very hot stone. When the kernels popped, they flew into the air. The waiting snackers had to be quick to catch the flying popcorn.

WHAT THEY WORE

The Aztecs liked bright colors and they found ways to add color to their clothing. They used vegetables and animals to create dyes for their thread and cloth. Brilliant scarlet came from certain insects that lived on prickly pear cacti. Dyes from shellfish produced rich purples, while indigo from plants dyed cloth dark blue. Depending on how they were used, dyes from brazilwood trees produced red, pink, or coral. Logwood could be used to dye cloth pink, blue, or green. Annatto seeds, from a tropical tree, turned cloth yellow, and iron oxide could be used to create blacks and rusty reds.

The cloth itself was made from agave fiber or cotton. Women spun the fiber into yarn or thread, then wove the cloth into fabric. All women were expected to know how to weave, but skilled weavers and dyers were in high demand.

Aztec commoners and slaves wore very few clothes. Cloth made from agave fiber was cheap, white, and long-wearing. Male slaves might only wear a cloth wrapped around their waist and between their legs, called a loincloth. If a man was a merchant or trader, the loincloth might have colorful embroidery.

Men also wore sleeveless cloaks made from agave for commoners or cotton for the nobility. These cloaks were usually rectangular,

CONNECTIONS

Hot Chocolate

The word *chocolate* is probably derived from the Nahuatl word *chocolatl*. Cocoa comes from the Aztec word *cacahuatl*. The original Aztec hot cocoa recipe was a mixture of ground cacao beans, water, and chili peppers. It was spicy, not sweet. And it was not always served hot.

The Spanish removed the peppers, heated the drink, and sweetened it with sugar. The British made another change—milk replaced the water.

and were sometimes worn by women as well. The cloak was called a *tilmatli*. Cloaks were dyed an array of different colors.

Many garments featured patterns or symbols woven into the fabric. Common symbols included the sun, seashells, fish, feathers, cacti, rabbits, and butterflies.

Women wore skirts (*cueitl*) that wrapped around their bodies. Loose blouses fell over the skirts. The blouses were sleeveless tunics, called *huipilli.* Wealthy women wore fancier clothes than poor women. They also had more clothing. Poor people rarely had more than one change of clothing.

Members of the noble class and religious leaders wore clothing that was heavily decorated, though similar in style to the clothes worn by commoners. Symbols of a noble's position were woven into or embroidered on clothing or in a headdress. Colors symbolized a person's status, so there were rules about the use of color. Priests wore black or dark green cloth, often embroidered with bones or skulls, symbolizing a priest's role in human sacrifices. The *tlatoani* was the only one allowed to wear teal or turquoise (two shades of blue).

Gold, silver, and turquoise were often used to decorate clothing and hair. Nobles wore necklaces, earrings, pendants, and bracelets. The use of feathers, furs, and other forms of decoration was common, but only the highest nobles could wear the brilliant green feathers of the quetzal.

GIRLS AND WOMEN

Women in the Aztec world were expected to be hardworking, clean, and do whatever was necessary to run the household. Some, however, took on jobs outside the home, serving as priestesses, doctors, and vendors in the markets.

Most practical training for girls from the commoner class, the *macehualli*, took place at home. The first lessons dealt with cloth. At 4 years old, girls began to learn how to spin thread. By 14, they were

Aztec clothing was often brilliantly dyed with colors taken from nature.

learning how to weave. During their lives, women would be responsible for spinning yarn, weaving and dying cloth, and for making, washing, and repairing clothes. Cloth was not only used for clothing, but also to pay tribute. Any extra cloth produced was a form of wealth that could be traded for other household goods. A daughter who could weave fine cloth was worth much to her family.

Girls also needed to learn their manners and obey their elders. Young girls did not disagree with their elders or complain about work. A girl's moral outlook on life was important. No man wanted to marry a woman who was not kind, obedient, honest, respectful, and skilled in making a home.

Once a girl reached 12 or 13 years old, she could easily run a household. Girls of this age knew how to grind corn into dough, form it into tortillas, and cook meals. They could weave, dye, and sew cloth into clothing. They knew how to clean the home, care for children, and shop in the market.

Fancy Footwear

Many Aztecs went barefoot much of the time. Sandals were the only type of shoes worn. *Cactli* were sandals with fiber or leather soles, a woven upper portion, and laces that wrapped around the ankle and calf to keep the shoes in place.

The sandals Aztec nobles wore for everyday wear were huaraches, much like those found in shoe stores today. The soles were single pieces of leather, with woven strips of leather on top. Nobles added decorations of precious metals or stones, or the skins of wild animals, such as jaguars. Some added bright feathers to their footgear.

Between 12 and 15, girls joined boys at the neighborhood *cuicacalli* ("house of song"). At this school, they learned to dance, sing, and play musical instruments. These talents were important for family gatherings and religious events. By learning these skills, the students also learned more about their culture and what was expected of them when they became adults.

Girls of the noble class, the *pipilti*, also needed to know how to clean, weave, and cook. They also learned singing, dancing, and music. One option open to a noble's daughter that was not open to common girls was becoming a priestess.

Once a woman of the *macehualli* class was married, her life took on a certain routine. Women rose at sunrise or before and went to bed at sunset. Early in the morning, they built a fire in the hearth. The first meal was corn porridge, and it was eaten every day. Women spent their mornings doing the tasks they learned as girls: washing, cleaning, childcare, cooking, and making cloth or clothing.

The Aztecs ate three meals a day, so cooking and cleaning took up many hours. The biggest meal was at noon, followed by more work and a light supper. Women who lived on a farm might work both in the home and in the fields—a double load, because men did not work around the house.

Noble women had less work to do. A woman with a wealthy or powerful husband usually had servants to do the housework and the cooking. She was ultimately responsible for her home, though, and supervised the work of her servants. Such a woman might spend her afternoons visiting with other wealthy women.

The wife or daughter of a merchant might be expected to help sell goods in the marketplace. Some women were professional marketers;

others just sold the extra products of their households. Women who were expert weavers or dyers might also have a chance to sell their work and earn extra money.

One other professional option for a woman was the job of a midwife. Midwives helped women give birth. Many also learned how to be healers. They learned which herbs could be used to cure sickness, how to set broken bones, and how to stitch wounds.

IN THEIR OWN WORDS

Advice for Girls

Huehuetlatolli can be translated as "sayings of the elders." It is a collection of advice that represents the Aztecs' ideals, and includes speeches and sayings for every occasion. The Huehuetlatolli were collected and written down by Juan Bautista (ca. 1535–1590), a priest and historian. Bautista was a great-grandson of Nezahualcoyotl and was Spanish on his father's side.

Here is a section that offers advice for girls.

Don't be careless, don't be negligent, don't fall behind, you who are my jewel, you who are my quetzal feather. . . . Attend carefully to the water and the grinding stone. And take hold of and lift up the sauce bowl and the basket. Lay them and carry them in front of people, next to people. Don't throw them down and break them, don't lay them down recklessly. You're to lay them down carefully and calmly. And you're not to go around like a crazy person, you're not to go around panting and laughing, you're not to go looking up ahead and from side to side, you're not to go looking all around at people, you're not to look people in the face. You're just to go straight ahead,

you're just to look straight ahead, when you go in front of people or pass people or meet people, so that you will acquire honor and respect there, so that no one will bother you, nor will you bother anyone else, and so that hospitality and respect will exist in moderation. And sing well, speak well, address people well, answer people well, make requests well. Speech is not something to be bought and sold. . . .

And lower your head, bow down before other people, beside other people. Show respect and deference to others. Don't offend them. Go about calmly and tranquilly. Show people love, ask them for things, be kind to them, give them a little something. Don't give people nasty looks, don't be greedy. . . .

And don't torment anyone, don't do harm to anyone, don't make fun of anyone, for then it is you who'll be tormented. And don't devote yourself to or divert yourself with wickedness. . . .

(Source: Bautista, Juan. *Huehuetlatolli.* Translated by Louise M. Burkhart. Personal correspondence, September 25, 2008. From Mexico: M. Ocharte (printer), 1600.)

MARRIAGE

Marriage was an important ritual for the Aztecs and included the families of both the bride and groom. When a young man reached the age for marriage—late teens or early 20s—his family met with his schoolmasters. This was a formal meal—a kind of ritual graduation ceremony. The parents announced that their son would no longer attend classes. Instead, the young man's parents looked for a wife for their son.

Several women who were in their late teens might be considered. It was up to the young man's parents and other relatives to choose one. The bride might be a woman the groom already knew or a complete stranger. Once the bride was chosen, women from the young man's family were sent to the bride's home to ask for her hand in marriage. The decision was left to her family, not to the bride.

There were an endless number of tasks that needed to be done before the actual ceremony took place. The family consulted a fortuneteller to determine a good day for the marriage. The young couple needed to be married under a favorable sign if the marriage was to be successful. The bride's family collected cocoa, flowers, tobacco and pipes, and corn to make tamales.

On the day before the wedding, a feast took place at the bride's home. To get ready for the feast, the bride bathed and washed her hair. She dressed in a heavily embroidered blouse and skirts and wore red feathers on her body. She wore makeup, which might have been the only time she did so during her life. That night, both families went to the groom's home, where the wedding would take place.

The wedding took place by the family hearth. There was singing, dancing, and feasting. In the same way that brides and grooms today share bits of wedding cake, the bride and groom fed each other tamales. Then the pair went to their room, where they prayed together for four days.

The newly married couple received gifts of food, household goods, pottery, and other items. Then they would usually move in with the husband's family. However, the household structure was so flexible that they could end up in their own household, living with other relatives, or even living with the wife's parents. Since women usually married within their *calpulli*, they rarely ended up far from their parents' home.

BIRTH AND BABIES

The purpose of every marriage was to produce children. The bride's primary task was to become a mother. The couple wanted sons because

Tying the Knot

In the United States and other English-speaking lands, people sometimes say that when two people marry, they "tie the knot." In an Aztec wedding ceremony, people did not say this, but they did act it out. Part of the bride's blouse and the groom's cloak were tied together, showing they were now joined as husband and wife.

Keeping Them Close

The Aztecs believed that if young girls ate while they were standing up, they would end up marrying someone who took them far from their home. Since most parents wanted their daughters close by, they always made sure the girls ate sitting down.

sons took care of their parents when they got old. Sons could take over a business, a trade, or farmland.

Aztec families loved their children. Each birth was a blessing, and each child was treasured. When a woman reached her seventh or eighth month of pregnancy, a midwife came to help her from that time through the delivery of her baby. Midwives made sure pregnant mothers were well fed and healthy.

When the baby was born, the midwife blessed the baby and honored the new mother for her bravery and strength. The cutting of the

IN THEIR OWN WORDS

The Warrior Mother

The Aztecs believed that giving birth was as much a battle as warfare was for men. A "victory" meant the birth of a healthy baby. Women who were "defeated"—who lost their lives in childbirth—were considered as noble as men who died in battle. Here is part of the ceremony midwives performed after a woman successfully gave birth.

> O my daughter, O valiant woman, you
>   worked, you toiled.
> You soared like an eagle, you sprang like a
>   jaguar,
> you put all your strength behind the shield;
>   you endured.
>
> You went forth into battle, you emulated
>   our Mother Cihuacoatl Quilaztli,
> and now our lord has seated you on the
>   Eagle Mat, the Jaguar Mat.
> You have spent yourself, O my daughter,
>   now be tranquil.

Emulated means "copied" and tranquil means "calm." Cihuacoatl Quilaztli was a goddess who, along with Quetzalcoatl, helped create the human race. The eagle and the jaguar were two sacred animals to the Aztecs.

The midwife also spoke if the woman died in childbirth. Here is part of her blessing. The last two lines suggest the Aztecs' belief that the dead mother would live forever as a goddess.

> O My little one, my daughter, my
>   beloved mistress,
> you have wearied yourself, manfully you
>   have fought.
> By your labors, you have won our Lord's
>   noble death, glorious death. . .
> Eternally, you shall live and joy and
>   gladness
> next to, beside, our mistress, the divine
>   woman.

(Source: Knabb, T. J., editor. *A Scattering of Jades: Stories, Poems, and Prayers of the Aztecs.* Translated by Thelma D. Sullivan. New York: Touchstone Books, 1994.)

Taking on Responsibility

Girls began spinning thread at age 4, sweeping at 12, grinding maize at 13, and weaving at 14. At 4, a boy might be responsible for fetching water. He learned how to fish at age 6, and a 14-year-old boy might be fishing on his own from a canoe.

umbilical cord was important. A boy's cord was given to warriors to take to a battlefield, so they could bury it there. This act symbolized the boy's future role as a warrior. A girl's cord was buried by the hearth. These two events symbolized the lives of adults: men as warriors, women as cooks and keepers of the sacred hearth.

Aztec parents called in a fortuneteller as soon as a child was born. That person arrived with the *tonalamatl*, the Book of Days. The fortuneteller decided which signs would influence the child's life. Then the fortuneteller set a date and time for the baby's naming. This would usually be four days after the birth.

On the fourth day, the family held a ritual bathing ceremony. The bath took place on a mat made of reeds. Items that would be important in the child's life were placed on the mat. For a girl, the items might be a spindle used for spinning thread, pots and pans, and foods. For a boy, the items would relate to a craft or trade: farm tools for a farmer, weapons for a warrior, and so on. The baby was washed and raised to the sky in each direction. The midwife gave the baby his or her name. Children then ran through the village calling out the baby's new name.

Mothers raised their children to follow the customs of the time. Children were taught from birth that they must behave well and do as they were told. Up to the age of 3 or 4, children played in the home. They had simple toys—dolls for girls and tools or weapons for boys. Education started early. Young people were trained from age 4 to meet their responsibilities to the family, the *calpulli*, and the Aztec Empire.

EDUCATION

Aztec children were expected to go to school when they came of age. The actual age when they went is not clear. It could be as young as 7 or as old as 14 or 15. The school a student attended depended on social class and gender. The basic education of a boy was through his father and the school. For a girl, her main teacher was her mother.

Children of the *macehualtin* class went to a local school. This school, the *telpochcalli* ("youth house"), was usually next door to or attached to the local temple. The boys learned trade skills, got military training, and learned how to be good citizens. They also learned the history of the Aztec Empire and the basic elements of the Aztec religion. Schooling for girls in the *macehualtin* class included dancing, singing, playing a musical instrument, and the basic elements of good citizenship. This took place before the girl was old enough to get married.

Children of the nobility attended a *calmecac*. Girls and boys went to separate schools, where they learned the responsibilities of being nobles. This included Aztec history, how to govern the lower classes, and fulfilling their responsibilities to the empire. The schools were run by priests and were attached to temples. Many boys who went to the *calmecac* were expected to become managers, either of their own land or in the Aztec cities.

Boys of the *macehualtin* class who were gifted or talented might attend a *calmecac*. Those sons would be destined to have better careers than their fathers.

At age 15, boys moved on to further studies in the *calmecac* or attended a *cuicacalli*. At the *calmecac*, the students took on added religious responsibilities. They also learned astronomy, poetry, writing, and mathematics. Students with talent in art might be pointed toward a career in architecture (designing buildings). Others might learn about the law or advanced ideas in farming. At the *cuicacalli*, the students learned singing and dancing.

The Aztecs used a form of hieroglyphics for writing. The glyphs were symbols that represented real objects. These might be people, animals, weather events, crops, or other items that appear in daily life. All cultures that lived in Mexico before the arrival of the Spanish used some form of hieroglyphic writing.

Documents were all handwritten. The job of *tlacuilo* (writer or scribe) was honored. There was no printing, and the Aztecs did not have books like the ones published today. But they did produce written documents. Book-length works were written on bark paper and folded up like an accordion.

CONNECTIONS

A Modern *Telpochcalli*

Chicago has the second-largest Mexican-American population of any U.S. city (Los Angeles has the largest). In one part of the city, officials have started their own version of a *telpochcalli.* Almost all of the students trace their roots to Mexico, and they learn a great deal about Mexican art and culture. Classes are conducted in both English and Spanish. They also celebrate certain Mexican holidays, such as the Day of the Dead. After classes, they can learn Mexican folk dances. Some of these dances have Aztec roots.

IN THEIR OWN WORDS

Advice for Boys

The Aztec elders offered advice on how a young man should behave. Here is an excerpt. It was written down by Spanish priest Andrés de Olmos (ca. 1485–1571). (Maguey is another name for agave, a plant grown for its strong fibers.)

Act! Cut wood, work the land,
Plant cactus, sow maguey;
You shall have drink, food, clothing.
With this you will stand straight.
With this you shall live.
For this you shall be spoken of, praise;
In this manner you will show yourself to your parents
and relatives.

(Source: León-Portilla, Miguel. *Aztec Thought and Culture.* Norman, Okla.: University of Oklahoma Press, 1963.)

After the Spanish conquest, a handful of books were written that recount the history and culture of the Aztecs before the Spanish arrived. They were written in Nahuatl and some also had notes in Spanish. In addition, many manuscripts were produced that combined pictures with Nahuatl text written using the European alphabet. The Aztecs learned to use the European alphabet and were writing their own chronicles, letters, and other documents in it by the 1540s.

These later Aztec works are called *codices* (*codex* is the singular). These codices were bound on the side, like regular books. All were sent back to Europe, where they were kept as curiosities. Today, they are named after the cities in Europe where they are now located or after the people responsible for collecting them.

SPORTS AND GAMES

Games were popular among nobles and commoners, and they liked to bet on the outcome. Most Aztec games had a religious or community purpose. Some games, such as the Aztec ball game, could be part of a ritual ceremony. The most popular Aztec game was *tlachtli,* a ball game with either two opponents or two opposing teams. *Tlachtli* is sometimes translated as simply "the ball game." Only nobles played the game. Ball games often took place as part of the ritual leading up to human sacrifices.

Tlachtli was played on a field bounded by two walls. The court was shaped like an "I" and measured 210 feet long and 35 feet wide. The goal of the game was to shoot a ball through a stone ring. The ball weighed about 9 pounds and was made of solid rubber. Contestants could use only their feet, knees, and hips to shoot the ball. No players could touch the ball with their hands. Players wore loincloths and a wide leather belt or girdle designed to protect the body from harm. The first team to put the ball through the ring won.

Tlachtli was a major spectator sport. The public was allowed to attend, and Aztecs bet heavily on the outcome. Nobles bet gold, precious stones, cloth, and feathers. They also bet slaves and land. People could bet their personal freedom, committing themselves to slavery if they lost their bet.

The Aztecs also played games of chance. *Patolli* was like a dice game, played with marked beans. The game was played on a stone table that was shaped like a cross. The end of each branch of the cross had a space, and play began in the middle, or home base. The cross was divided into squares, and markers were moved according to the throw of the dice. If a person got two dots, he or she moved the marker two spaces.

Pieces moved around the grid. A complete circuit of the grid allowed the player to remove his or her own piece from play. The opponent had to pay one marker to the player whenever a piece was removed from play. The game ended when one player lost all his or her markers.

CONNECTIONS

Do You Speak Nahuatl?

Starting in 2008, children in Mexico City were required to learn a second language in the classroom—Nahuatl, the language of the Aztecs. Although only a tiny percentage of the 20 million people in Mexico City speak Nahuatl, the government wants the children of Mexico City to be proud of their heritage.

Nahuatl was once spoken by everyone in the Aztec Empire. But now, authorities believe that less than 1 percent of Mexico City's population speaks Nahuatl. They hope to increase that number. Already, Mexican colleges offer courses in Nahuatl, and across Mexico, more than 1 million people speak it.

Most English-speaking people may not realize that they already know several Nahuatl words. *Coyote, tomato, avocado,* and *chili* come from Nahuatl, as does that most delicious of words—*chocolate.*

OLD AGE AND DEATH

The Aztecs honored people who lived to an old age. The elderly were considered wise, and their family and *calpulli* sought their advice. They sat on the local council—a political group that governed the *calpulli.* Much like grandparents today, they would warn their children and grandchildren about the problems one might face in life.

The elderly demanded and received respect from all. Elderly warriors received aide from the government, included housing and money for food.

The Aztec religion offered elders a way to prepare for their death. If they had committed some serious crime or sin, for example, they could make a formal confession. Although Aztec laws carried harsh treatments for crimes, a confession provided the confessor with protection. Such a confession usually occurred when people were very old or knew they were about to die, since they could only confess once during their lifetime.

Dead bodies would be either buried or cremated (burned). The treatment depended on how a person died. People who drowned were always buried. Death from certain diseases, such as leprosy, gout, or dropsy, along with the unusual death by a lightning strike, also required burial. Women who died while giving birth were honored and buried in the temple cemetery. Death by any other means meant cremation.

Fans packed the seats on the side of this court where the ball game known as *tlachtli* was played.

An Aztec Confession

Confessions were made to a diviner—a person who could understand the gods' wishes. The diviner for a confession served the goddess Tlazolteotl.

After confessing their wrong actions, the confessors had to fast (not eat for a long period), perform a bloodletting, then go at night to one of the shrines built for women who died during childbirth. The confessors wore only a paper skirt decorated with designs associated with Tlazolteotl.

They left the skirt behind at the shrine— a symbol that they had left behind their sins. They then went home naked in the dark. Being naked in public was considered shameful, so this was a serious way to show remorse!

The deaths of nobles were treated differently from the deaths of commoners. When a nobleman died, his wives and servants could choose to join him in that death. However, this was not required.

The nobleman's body was washed, dressed in fine clothes, and bound in a crouched position. Binding cloths held the body in that position. Then the body was cremated until nothing was left but ashes. The ashes were placed in a jar, along with a piece of jade, and the jar was buried under the floor of the person's home.

CHAPTER 6

RELIGION, ART, AND SCIENCE

RELIGION, ART, LITERATURE, AND MUSIC WERE CLOSELY linked in the Aztec world. The Aztecs had a complex religion with hundreds of gods and goddesses and a wide variety of rituals. Many Aztec beliefs and the gods connected to those beliefs were taken from cultures that had been conquered at earlier times. The Aztecs sometimes chose to worship the other peoples' gods instead of forcing the conquered people to worship theirs.

The Aztecs believed that the gods influenced every aspect of a person's life, from birth to death. They thought that personal tragedy was the punishment of the gods, just as thunder, lightning, too much or too little rain, sickness, and famine were direct results of unhappy gods.

Today, human sacrifice is probably the best-known part of the Aztec religion. But it was not as common as some sources claim. In addition to human sacrifice, people also offered the gods food, sporting events, dramatic festivals, and bloodletting. It was a common practice at certain religious events for priests and commoners to pierce their skin with cactus spines and offer their blood to the gods.

The Aztecs built massive temples specifically for holding sacrifices. Each temple, called a *teocalli*, had sacred pools for ritual bathing, gardens, and housing for priests. The human hearts and flesh offered were seen as food for the gods. Making sacrifices was one way to win the gods' favor so they would continue to help the Aztecs thrive as a people. A sacrifice might have just one victim, a few had many more, but very few took the lives of hundreds of captives. While many sacrifice victims were people captured in war, they were not always men. Women, children, and slaves could also be sacrificed. To remind the people and the

OPPOSITE
Tlaloc, the god of rain and water, was one of many gods in the Aztec culture.

How Is It Pronounced?

Chalchiuhtlicue
chahl-chew-TLEE-kway

Chicomecoatl
chee-koh-may-KOH-ahtl

Coatlicue
koh-ahtl-EE-kway

Teocalli
tay-oh-KAH-lee

The Whistle of Death

More than 15 years ago, archaeologists found a human skeleton buried in an Aztec temple. The skeleton held a skull-shaped whistle made of clay in each bony hand.

In the summer of 2008, musician Roberto Velazquez, an expert in the sounds made by the peoples of Mexico before the Spanish arrived, made an exact replica of the whistle, and blew into it. The shrill, windy screech made his spine tingle.

Velazquez is one of many researchers looking into how the Aztecs may have used music and other sounds in their lives. "We've been looking at our ancient culture as if they were deaf and mute," says Velazquez (quoted in "Recreating the Sound of Aztec Whistles of Death," CNN.com). "I think all of this is closely tied to what they did, how they thought." Experts think that these whistles of death may have been blown by victims before they were sacrificed on the temple altars, to aid them on their journey into the afterlife.

gods of the sacrifices made, temples had racks to display the cleaned skulls of those sacrificed.

REACHING THE AFTERLIFE

The Aztecs believed in an afterlife—a form of life after death. The quality of that afterlife did not depend on how a person behaved during their life. An Aztec's destination in the afterlife depended on how the person died.

The person's body or ashes remained on earth, while the soul began the voyage to one of several afterworlds. Sacrifice victims and warriors who died in battle immediately went to join Huitzilopochtli, the god of sun and war. The dead warriors were said to travel with the sun as it moved through the sky from dawn to noon. The warriors' souls stayed in the eastern paradise for four years and then returned to earth as hummingbirds.

Women who died while giving birth to their first baby—if the child had not yet been born before they died—went to the western part of the sun's paradise. These women escorted the sun as it moved from noon to sunset. They also returned to earth on certain days, then went back to the western sky. When they came back, they caused children to become sick and haunted their former husbands.

People who died from drowning, lightning, and diseases associated with water were buried and went to Tlalocan, the paradise of the rain gods. The rain god, Tlaloc, selected certain individuals and sent these deaths to them on purpose. Children sacrificed to Tlaloc also arrived here.

Spirits of children who died while still breast-feeding went to the highest heaven, where the creator god and goddess lived. These children were still considered innocent and pure. They sucked milk from the blossoms of a great tree until they could be sent to earth as new babies.

Everyone who did not go to the afterworlds already described ended up in the underworld, called Mictlan. The journey into Mictlan was difficult. But once there, it was not a bad or punishing place. If anything, Mictlan was just boring.

The Long Road to Rest

The dead faced a long, difficult journey to reach the afterworld of Mictlan. The souls journeying there went through nine steps, and the trip took four years. A soul had to:

1. cross a deep river called Apanohuaya
2. pass between Tepetl Monamictia, two mountains that were joined together
3. climb an obsidian mountain called Itztepetl
4. go through eight gorges and eight valleys, where icy winds cut like knives
5. be pierced by arrows, which was called Temiminaloyan
6. travel among wild creatures that ate human hearts
7. enter a place with waving flags where they were met by a lizard called Xochitonatl; this lizard signaled the end of the journey was near
8. cross nine rivers called Chiconahuapan
9. finally reach the place of rest in Mictlan

A decorated human skull honors Tezcatlipoca, one of the Aztec creator gods.

GODS AND GODDESSES

The Aztecs honored three major gods who were important forces in their lives. Beneath those three gods was a second level of gods, then a third, and hundreds of gods filled the lesser ranks. The responsibilities of gods overlapped, and many gods were in charge of more than one area. There were several war gods, for example. Each had other responsibilities, and while one might be responsible for victory, another tricked humans into going to war.

The three primary gods were Huitzilopochtli, Tezcatlipoca, and Quetzalcoatl. Huitzilopochtli's name means "hummingbird left." Huitzilopochtli was the god of the sun. His name refers to the position of the sun during the winter, when it is on the left as it crosses from east to west. He is identified with the winter dry season, which is the time for war. He was also the lord of the south, the lord of the day, and the patron god of the Aztec people. The Aztecs believed that Huitzilopochtli was in a constant struggle with the forces of the night to keep humans alive.

Tezcatlipoca, the "smoking mirror," was a war god as well. He was also the god of magic and death. His name comes from the black obsidian mirror he was said to carry. Tezcatlipoca was missing a foot, which was said to have been eaten by a monster as Tezcatlipoca dragged the earth from the waters and created the land. Tezcatlipoca could be impulsive and bad-tempered but he was not really evil. He sent things like hurricanes and temptation, but could also send good fortune and remove the effects of sin through the confession ritual.

Quetzalcoatl, the "quetzal-feathered serpent," was the god of civilization, priests, and learning or knowledge. This god was responsible for the Aztec story of creation. Quetzalcoatl took the form of the morning star, and his twin brother was the evening star (Venus). He battled the stars that filled the night sky and, finishing the battle at dawn, was the last star to retire before the sun rose.

Among the most powerful goddesses were Coatlicue, Chalchiuhtlicue, and Chicomecoatl. Like the gods, goddesses had many responsibilities.

In Nahuatl, Coatlicue means "the one with the skirt of serpents." She and several other goddesses were associated with the power of both the earth and women to create life. They were also associated with death and decay, since they give rise to new life. Coatlicue was the mother of the gods and the one who gave birth to the moon and stars. She was also the mother of Huitzilopochtli. Coatlicue was sometimes a mother, sometimes a grandmother, and always the patron goddess of women who die giving birth. She was shown with snakes in her skirts, wearing a necklace featuring human hearts, hands, and skulls. These images suggest that life is not always a beautiful thing and dangers sometimes await.

Chalchiuhtlicue, the "one with the skirt of precious jade," was the goddess of lakes, streams, and rivers. This goddess was sometimes shown with a river flowing from her. Chalchiuhtlicue was married to the god of rain, Tlaloc. She was the goddess who unleashed the great flood that ended the fourth world. This flood washed away the evil people of the earth. In Aztec mythology, the world began again and we are now in the fifth world.

Chicomecoatl, "seven-serpent," was the goddess of corn. Without her, the Aztecs thought there would be no corn—and most Aztecs ate corn in some form three times a day. Chicomecoatl was represented as a young woman wearing a necklace of golden ears of corn. She also held ears of corn that looked like feathers. Each fall, a young girl who was supposed to represent the goddess was sacrificed. The Aztecs believed that if Chicomecoatl appreciated the sacrifice, they would have a plentiful harvest.

THE AZTEC CALENDAR

The Aztecs had an excellent understanding of astronomy, the study of the movements of the stars and planets. They mapped the movements of these heavenly bodies and realized the clear relationship between these movements and the passage of time.

The Aztec calendar was far more complex than the calendar used today. In fact, they had two calendars that followed separate cycles. One calendar covered 365 days. It had 18 months that lasted 20 days each, with a five-day period at the end to even out the year. The five-day period was believed to be highly unlucky, and it was expected that disasters would occur during this evil time.

The Rabbit in the Moon

When they looked at the moon, Europeans thought they could see a person's face—the "man in the moon." The Aztecs saw something completely different—a rabbit.

According to an Aztec legend, when the moon first appeared, it was as bright as the sun. The gods wanted to make a clear distinction between night and day, so one of them threw a rabbit against the moon to make it darker. The rabbit struck hard, and its body left a permanent mark. The face of the moon was bruised and the dark, rabbit-shaped mark has remained for all time.

The Months of the Aztec 365-Day Calendar

MONTH	NAME	PATRON GOD(S)	REQUIRED RITES
1	Atlcahualo (stopping water)	Tlaloc, Chachihutlicue	Children sacrificed to the water gods
2	Tlacaxipehualiztli (flaying people)	Xipe Totec	Priests dance, men flayed, warriors sacrificed
3	Tozoztontli (the little vigil)	Coatlicue, Tlaloc	Flayed skin buried, children sacrificed
4	Hueytozoztli (the great vigil)	Centeotl, Chicomecoatl	New maize blessed, maidens sacrificed
5	Toxcatl (the dry time)	Tezcatlipoca, Huitzilopochtli	Ritual performers sacrificed to the major gods
6	Etzalcualiztli (meal of maize and beans)	Tlaloque	Human sacrifice by drowning, ritual bathing
7	Tecuilhuitontli (small feast)	Huixtocihuatl, Xochipilli	Impersonators of the gods sacrificed
8	Huey tecuilhuitl (the great feast)	Xilonen	Feast of the young corn, lords offer gifts and foods for commoners

Each Aztec month had a name, patron gods responsible for overseeing the time, and demands on the Aztec people. The Aztec 365-day calendar was both a way of keeping track of time and a list of religious responsibilities.

The other calendar was a religious calendar. It covered 260 days and was called the *tonalpohualli*, or the count of days.

The *tonalpohualli* can be thought of as two linked wheels. Each of the 20 days of the month that appeared on one wheel had an individual name. The day names were snake, lizard, house, wind, crocodile, flower, rain, flint, movement, vulture, eagle, jaguar, cane, grass, monkey, dog,

9	Tlaxochimaco (laying flowers)	Huitzilopochtli	Gods decorated with flower wreaths, feasts of cornmeal cakes and turkey
10	Xocotl huetzi (the fall of fruit)	Xiuhtecutli	Victims sacrificed to the fire gods by being burned alive
11	Ochpaniztli (sweeping roads)	Tlazolteotl	Sweeping houses and roads
12	Teotleco (descent of the gods)	Tezcatlipoca	Welcoming the gods' return to earth, sacrifices by fire
13	Tepeilhuitl (feast of the hills)	Tlaloc	Honoring the rain gods, human sacrifices, cannibalism
14	Quecholli (precious feather)	Mixcoatl-Camaxtli	Hunting and fasting, sacrificial games, feasting
15	Panquetzaliztli (raising the banner)	Huitzilopochtli	Homes and fruit trees decorated with banners, many human sacrifices
16	Atemoztli (water falling)	Tlaloc	Feast honoring the water god, children and slaves sacrificed
17	Tititl (stretching)	Ilamatecuhtli	Magic to bring more rain, women beaten until they cry
18	Izcalli (resuscitation)	Xiuhtecuhtli	Feasting on tamales stuffed with green vegetables
19	Nemontemi (the empty days)	None	Five days considered unlucky, no rites or rituals

water, rabbit, deer, and skull (death). Each name had a specific glyph that appeared on the calendar. On the second wheel were the numbers 1 to 13. When the two wheels moved together, each day name appeared next to a number. The numbers continued to repeat until the 20 day names and 13 numbers reached 260 days, marking the complete religious calendar.

Once every 52 years, the 260-day calendar and the 365-day calendar ended on the same day and then started again. Thus, the Aztecs divided time by groups of 52 years. This time grouping would be similar to the modern concept of centuries.

The Calendar Stone

The Aztecs who lived in Tenochtitlan had no need for a calendar hung on the wall. They had the Calendar Stone—a carved, circular stone calendar that weighed 24 tons and measures 12 feet across and 3 feet thick. It was carved from a single piece of basalt rock.

The Calendar Stone was buried under rubble when the Spanish conquered Tenochtitlan. It remained hidden for 250 years. Then, in 1790, workers making repairs to the cathedral in Mexico City found the stone. It is now kept in Mexico City's National Museum of Anthropology.

The stone is not really a calendar, but a visual image of the Aztecs' view of the cosmos and time. In the stone's center is the face of Tlaltecuhtli, the earth goddess. She is looking up through the solar disk (the stone would have been placed flat on the ground). She is associated with the fifth creation or age, which goes by the calendar name Four Motion. Surrounding Tlaltecuhtli are the signs associated with the four creations that came before the current one.

The earth goddess Tlaltecuhtli is at the center of this massive calendar stone, which illustrates the Aztec conception of time and space.

The carvings on the stone are highly detailed. They feature the 20 animals associated with the days of the month in the 260-day calendar. The stone also shows serpents and scenes of the four worlds said to have existed before present-day earth. The intricate artwork of the stone is even more amazing considering the fact that the Aztecs had only stone tools.

ARTS AND CRAFTS

The Aztecs had no iron or bronze tools. They relied on bone, wooden, and stone tools to create the items needed for daily life and their art. The stones used were obsidian, a naturally occurring volcanic glass, and chert, a hard, dark rock. They made blades, sharpening tools, and drills from these materials. Using these tools, the Aztecs created massive stone carvings as well as small, detailed figures.

Many excellent examples of Aztec carving are on display in Mexico City's National Museum of Anthropology. A statue of Coatlicue is one example of large Aztec art. The statue is nearly nine feet high and is incredibly detailed. The goddess's necklace of hearts and hands and her skirt of snakes are precisely carved.

The Aztecs created art as a form of religious expression and a way to honor their gods. Some Aztec art featured pictographs—pictures that represent words, ideas, or sounds. Common pictographs range from jaguars and snakes to beetles and representations of lightning or wind. They sometimes appear on temple walls.

Statues were mostly made of stone, although small figures carved from jade and quartz have been found in Aztec ruins. Other large statues were made of clay. Some statues were freestanding, while others were reliefs—they projected out from the sides of buildings. Both kinds decorated temples. Stone sculptures represented popular gods or the victims sacrificed to those gods. In addition to the gods, artisans carved figures of humans and animals.

Aztec artists also made paintings and drawings. The pictures of the gods were not realistic, but were meant to symbolize things about them. Bright colors were used in these paintings. Paints were made by grinding materials found in nature—such as stones, shells, and plants—into a fine powder and mixing them with oil. Bright orange, yellow, red, green, and blue are typical Aztec paint colors.

Aztec craftsmen created masks and warrior art for use in religious ceremonies. Making masks was a skilled craft that was in great demand. Masks were worn for many religious rituals. The masks of warriors were

Throwing Out the Pots

Archaeologists have learned about ancient Aztec pottery thanks to one of their customs: When a 52-year calendar cycle came to an end, all household goods were destroyed. By studying pieces of broken pottery and whole pots that were thrown away, archaeologists have learned about changes in Aztec art.

The Aztec Bestiary

A bestiary is basically a catalog of animals. The Aztecs created their own bestiary in the form of statues. Existing Aztec statues represent the animals common to their fields and forests: jaguars, coyotes, dogs, eagles, turkey buzzards, snakes, and ducks. There are also statues of toads and frogs, fish, and even insects.

The animals are carved from stone and semi-precious gems. After the Spanish arrived, copper was also sometimes used. Many statues are on display in the National Museum of Anthropology in Mexico City, and in traveling exhibits throughout the world.

Motecuhzoma's Headdress

An elaborate feathered headdress has long been associated with Motecuhzoma II. It includes 400 green quetzal feathers and gold ornaments. This headdress was said to be worn by Motecuhzoma II, but more likely it was given to Spain's King Charles V as a gift. The headdress was then thought to have been passed on to several different European nobles before ending up in the Museum of Ethnology in the Austrian capital of Vienna.

In 2006, the Mexican government asked Austria to give back the headdress. Even though it most likely never belonged to Motecuhzoma, it is the only known Aztec headdress in the world and is an important part of Mexican culture. Under Austrian law, however, the Vienna museum is not allowed to let others borrow it or to give it away. The headdress remains in Vienna.

designed to frighten the enemy. In addition to masks, ceremonial costumes also included headdresses, or large, fancy headgear. Most headdresses and many items of clothing for religious events featured feathers, and the Aztecs had feather artists to produce these works of art.

Few of the exquisite featherwork headdresses and outfits made for nobles and priests still exist. The fragile feathers are not easily preserved, and so Aztec featherwork is not very well known. The *amantecatl*, or feather artist, crafted unique works that were visually brilliant and dynamic.

Feather artists collected feathers from throughout the empire. They glued the feathers onto a backing that was supported by a framework. The feathers used were from the brilliantly colored tropical birds of the region. Once finished, a feather headdress or cloak was a remarkably beautiful work of art.

Weaving was also considered an art, although all Aztec women could weave cloth. Even though the skill was common, there were women whose work was exceptional. A weaver with great skill was a woman of great worth to her family and her *calpulli*. Designs and colors woven into the cloth told where a person came from and that person's status in society. Cloth gave clues to the religion, hunting styles, important gods, and people in the culture. Today archaeologists use these clues to learn the age of cloth and which people produced it.

Cloth was used for warmth (clothing) and for rituals (sacrifice). It could also be used as a form of currency. In the Aztec markets, lengths of cloth were an important part of the trading system. Cloth could pay for a basket of dried corn, leather for sandals, or fruit. It could also pay the tax collector.

Cotton was the most valuable fabric used by the Aztecs, but they also wove cloth from fibers taken from the agave plant and from palm fibers. Valuable weavings were used as offerings to the gods. They draped the inner rooms of temples and palaces. They wrapped newborn babies and the dead before burial or cremation. A bride might bring cloth as a form of payment called a dowry, which went to her new husband.

Pottery was a practical art form. Pots were used for cooking, storing, and serving food. Most Aztec pottery had red, black, white, or orange glazes. Typical Aztec pottery was not made on a potter's wheel but was molded by hand. Most pots featured designs related to the gods or to the *calpulli* to which the potter belonged. The district of Cholula was so well known for its superior red-and-black pottery that Motecuhzoma II refused to eat off any plates that were not made in Cholula.

IN THEIR OWN WORDS

The Feather Artist

The *Florentine Codex* is the name given to 12 books created under the supervision of Bernardino de Sahagún between approximately 1540 and 1585. One section of the *codex* explains the habits and skills that distinguish bad artisans from good ones. Here are some of the qualities of the good and bad feather artists.

Amantécatl: the feather artist.
He is whole; he has a face and a heart.
The good feather artist is skillful,
Is master of himself; it is his duty
To humanize the desires of the people.
He works with feathers,
chooses them and arranges them,
paints them with different colors,
joins them together.

The bad feather artist is careless;
He ignores the look of things,
He is greedy, he scorns other people.
He is like a turkey with a shrouded heart,
Sluggish, coarse, weak.
The things that he makes are not good.
He ruins everything that he touches.

(Source: León-Portilla, Miguel. *Aztec Thought and Culture.* Norman, Okla.: University of Oklahoma Press, 1963.)

LITERATURE

Aztec literature, like Aztec works of art, was based on religion. It explained creation, major events in nature, and the efforts of the

Aztec Writing

The Aztecs did not write words using letters. Instead, they wrote using glyphs—representations of things and ideas, much like the picture writing of the Egyptians. This system of writing is called hieroglyphics. The hieroglyphics told of great victories, brilliant warriors, human sacrifices, and events from Aztec daily life. They were carved into monuments and also written down in books.

gods on behalf of or opposed to human beings. Every god had his or her myths; every religious event had poetry and tales as part of the ritual.

Myths explained how the earth was formed and how people came to exist. The Aztecs believed that in the beginning, the world was ruled by darkness. Their world began with the coming of light. The universe also went through periods of birth, death, and rebirth.

The first age was called Four Water. In this period, the gods created humans from ashes and fed them acorns. Chalchiuhtlicue, the water goddess, ruled the first age, which ended when floods covered the world.

The second age was called Four Jaguar. During Four Jaguar, human beings were all giants. Tezcatlipoca ruled Four Jaguar, which ended when the sun fell from the sky and set the world on fire. In this dark world, the surviving people were eaten by jaguars.

The third age was called Four Rain. Tlaloc, the god of thunder, lightning, and rain, ruled the world of Four Rain.

The fourth age was called Four Wind and was ruled by Quetzal-coatl. This period ended when a terrible hurricane destroyed the land and blew all the people from the world. A few people survived by being changed into monkeys, and those monkeys hid in the forests.

Nanahuatzin ruled the fifth age, which is called Four Movement. The current world is the fifth age. Four Movement began when Nanahuatzin threw himself into a fire and became the sun. It will end with earthquakes.

Aztec poetry covered the basic themes of nature, acts of heroism, nobles, and religious rites. In Aztec times, poetry was performed in public, usually accompanied by a melody. The Spanish called the Aztec poems *cantares*, which is the Spanish word for "songs" or "chants." The Nahuatl word is *cuicatl*.

Although many poems were recited as part of religious rituals, it was equally common to have poetry at banquets or victory feasts. The drums beat out the rhythm, dancers whirled about in colorful costumes, and the poet sang of love, bravery, nature, and sadness—all the same topics about which poets write and singers sing today.

Some of these poems might be considered epic poetry, which tells the stories of great heroes or important historical events. These include *Cuauhcuicatl* ("songs of the eagle") and *Yaocuicatl* ("warrior

The Aztec Creation Story

The Aztecs had several stories about how the world was created, taken in from the various peoples they conquered. One of these stories features Quetzalcoatl and Tezcatlipoca.

Quetzalcoatl and Tezcatlipoca looked down from their place in the sky and saw only water. As they watched, a gigantic goddess lay on the water. She had many mouths and was eating everything she could find. The two gods knew that if they created anything, the goddess would eat it. In an effort to stop her, they transformed themselves into two huge serpents and went down into the water. One of them grabbed the goddess by the arms while the other grabbed her around the legs. Before she could resist, they pulled until she broke apart. Her head and shoulders became the earth and the lower part of her body became the sky.

The other gods were angry at what Quetzalcoatl and Tezcatlipoca had done. They decided to make it up to the goddess for losing her arms and legs. They would create all the things people needed to survive from the rest of her body. From her hair they created trees, grass, and flowers. Her eyes were used to make caves, fountains, and wells. Rivers poured from her mouth. The hills and valleys that filled the land burst from her nose. Mountains rose up from her shoulders.

The goddess was still not happy, though. The people heard her cries in the night. She cried because she hungered for human blood and could not give people food unless she drank. So she is fed with the blood of humans and with their hearts. In turn, she feeds humans from the earth. There is no end to this cycle.

songs"). Other poetry focused on daily life. These include *Xochicuicatl* ("flower songs") and *Huehuecuicatl* ("songs of the elders"). Flower songs told about the beauty and pleasures of nature. There were songs about spring and the first sprouting of corn.

MUSIC AND DANCE

Music and dance accompanied most religious festivals, including human sacrifices. Drums set the beat for warriors to march to war and announced the celebration of victory. While war and sacrificial songs were most common, music also told the story of the Aztec culture. Songs

Official Records

Along with writing poetry and myths, the Aztecs produced many official records. The governing of an empire required a great deal of paperwork. Districts paid taxes. Merchants recorded sales and profits. Armies recorded victories. People owned land. And the Aztecs had many religious events. The Aztecs had scribes to keep records of their works. Each scribe had a specific area of knowledge, much like we have historians, accountants, and people who register births, deaths, and deeds. The Aztecs recorded so much information that Tenochtitlan used up 480,000 sheets of paper a year.

spoke of a family's ancestors and the acts of greatness that enabled the family to reach its current social position.

The Aztecs had many wind and percussion instruments but no string instruments. Their music was played on instruments made from wood, bones, skins, shells, and clay. Percussion instruments included rattles, shakers, and a variety of drums. Drums played a big part in the music of the Aztecs. The *ayotl* was a drum made from a turtle shell. Prongs were placed on the underside of the shell and struck to create sound. The *teponaztli* was a horizontal log drum that was played with mallets. The *huehuetl* was an upright skin drum, played with the hands like a bongo drum. A musician could make the *huehuetl* produce two tones by playing on the inner or outer area of the drum's skin. The *huehuetl* and *teponaztli* were played together for most Aztec songs.

Rattles were another form of percussion instrument. They were made by filling gourds or sticks with stones, seeds, or beads. Rattle sticks are still used in native Mesoamerican music. Maracas, used in modern Mexican music, are like the rattles of Aztec times.

Melodies were played on flutes or horns such as the *atecocoli*, a large conch shell that sounded much like a trumpet. The *chichitli* was a high-pitched whistle, somewhat like a piccolo. The Aztecs even had an instrument that made a buzzing sound, called the *cocoloctli*. The Aztec flute, the *huilacapitztli*, is still very popular in Mexico.

Every Aztec person learned the songs, instruments, and dances of their culture. Between the ages of 12 and 15, Aztec children went to the *cuicacalli*, where they learned singing and dancing.

When people gathered for a religious rite, the music provided the appropriate mood. Hundreds of people sang and danced together, from young children to the elderly. Musicians were extremely careful not to make any mistakes as they played. An error was a serious insult to the gods and might displease them.

Most nobles had their own orchestras, as well as songwriters and dancers. Spanish priest Gerónimo de Mendieta (1525–1604) wrote, "Each lord had in his house a chapel with composer-singers of dances and songs, and these were thought to be ingenious in knowing how to compose the songs in their manner of meter and the couplets that they had. Ordinarily they sang and danced in the principal festivities that were every 20 days, and also on other less principal occasions." (quoted in "Aztec Music" at Aztec-History.com).

Family celebrations and all religious rituals had music to mark the occasion. Special songs were written and sung for Huitzilopochtli, Tezcatlipoca, Tlaloc, and Ometeotl. Songs praised the gods and asked for their assistance, particularly in bringing rain or ending a famine.

ARCHITECTURE

Many ancient cultures, including the Aztecs, built step pyramids. These pyramids did not have smooth sides, like the famous ones in Egypt. Instead, the sides were like giant stone stairways. Often the pyramids were built in layers. Each added layer was slightly smaller than the one underneath, and the layers served as steps to the top of the pyramid.

IN THEIR OWN WORDS

The Flower Tree

Some of the poems said to be written by Nezahualcoyotl, the great king of Texcoco, were actually written by other people. In their works, the poets pretended to be the king or to be speaking for him. Here is an excerpt from a flower song called *The Flower Tree* that was once attributed to Nezahualcoyotl. The poet seems to be telling his listeners that since life is short, they must find beauty and pleasure when they can.

Begin the song in pleasure, singer, enjoy, give pleasure to all, even to Life Giver. Yyeo ayahui ohuaya.

Delight, for Life Giver adorns us. All the flower bracelets, your flowers, are dancing. Our songs are strewn in this jewel house, this golden house. The Flower Tree grows and shakes, already it scatters. . . .

Live here on earth, blossom! As you move and shake, flowers fall. My flowers are eternal, my songs are forever: I raise them: I, a singer. I scatter them, I spill them, the flowers become gold. . . .

Flowers of raven, flowers you scatter, you let them fall in the house of flowers. Ohuaya ohuyaya.

Ah, yes: I am happy, I prince Nezahualcoyotl, gathering jewels, wide plumes of quetzal, I contemplate the faces of jades: they are the princes! I gaze into the faces of Eagles and Jaguars, and behold the faces of jades and jewels! Ohuaya ohuyaya. . . .

We will pass away. I, Nezahualcoyotl, say, Enjoy! Do we really live on earth? . . .

Not forever on earth, only a brief time here! . . .

(Source: Curl, John, translator. *Ancient American Poets.* Tempe, Ariz.: Bilingual Review Press, 2005.)

This large Aztec drum is made of wood and decorated with carvings of birds and other creatures.

Temples were not open to the public. Other than priests and nobles, visitors tended to be sacrifice victims.

Aztec pyramids always had two staircases, and each set of stairs led to a different shrine. This way, each Aztec temple provided shrines for two different gods. The Great Temple in Tenochtitlan, for example, served both the god of the sun (Huitzilopochtli) and the god of rain (Tlaloc). The shrine to Huitzilopochtli was painted red and white, which symbolized war and sacrifice. The shrine to Tlaloc was decorated in white and blue, to symbolize rain and water.

The pyramid of the Great Temple rose 197 feet into the sky, or the equivalent of a 20-story building. Its height was a constant reminder to Aztecs that the gods commanded the heavens and were far above the ordinary people.

The temple was decorated with clay and stone figures that represented and honored Aztec gods. The Aztecs left offerings at the temple to gain the gods' favor, and archaeologists have recovered many of these gifts. The temple itself was torn down by the Spanish, but part of its ruins can be seen today in Mexico City.

CONNECTIONS

Imagining the Music of the Aztecs

Mexican composer Carlos Chavez (1899–1978) never heard Aztec music—no one in modern times has. But he knew the music of Indian people still living in Mexico during the 20th century. And he knew the kinds of instruments the Aztecs played.

With that knowledge, he composed "Xochipilli (An Imagined Aztec Music)." In this piece, the musicians play gourds, rattles, flutes, and drums similar to the ones the Aztecs played. A trombone, however, replaces the shell used as a horn.

Chavez's work was first played in New York City in 1940 and it is still performed today. It offers one artist's view of the kind of music that moved the Aztecs.

SCIENCE AND TECHNOLOGY

The Aztecs developed technology that suited a great empire. Among the culture's accomplishments were advances in mathematics, astronomy, timekeeping, weapons, and medicine.

The Aztecs created a system of mathematics to suit their needs. They used a system based on the number 20. Math was used in business, to determine the amount of tribute owed to the empire, and to record property measurements.

Writing Numbers, Aztec Style

The Aztecs had several different ways of writing numbers. They used dots to represent the numbers 1 through 19. Numbers larger than 19 featured dots and symbols.

Special symbols represented the numbers 20, 400, and 8,000. The Aztecs used flags for 20, feathers for 400, and incense bags for 8,000. Using that system, the number 867 would be written using seven vertical dots (7), three flags (60), and two feathers (400 x 2 = 800).

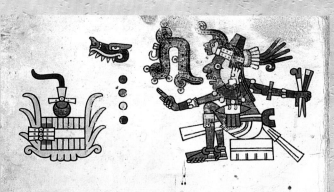

The dots and symbols beneath this drawing of a minor god are good examples of the lines and dots used in the Aztec numbering system.

A culture that went to war needed weapons. Axe blades were made from stone. Sharp knives and spear blades were made from obsidian. The Aztecs also developed a spear-thrower, an *atlatl.* This was a sling used to help propel the spear. It could also be used for fishing and hunting. An expert with the *atlatl* could bring down a deer.

Warriors made a kind of sword called a *macuahuitl* out of wood with an obsidian blade. It was used as a cutting weapon. It was sharp enough to cut off a person's head or kill a horse. The Aztecs also had bows and arrows for war and hunting.

AZTEC MEDICINE

The Aztecs made great advances in medicine. They used herbs for healing, and had an excellent understanding of the human body, health, and how the body heals. Healers could be either men or women.

The Aztecs used dozens of herbs either alone or combined with others. Some of the herbs could be poisonous if used in the wrong way or the wrong amount. An herbalist had to know exactly what he or she was doing.

The Aztecs believed that many illnesses were a direct result of unhappy or angry gods. They developed healing drinks, rubs, and ointments, and combined them with prayer, fasting, and sacrifices. The

CONNECTIONS

Healing Herbs

The knowledge of Aztec medicine was recorded in 1552 in a document called the *Badianus Manuscript.* It was written by Martín de la Cruz (dates unknown), an Aztec physician, and listed ointments and drinks used to treat a wide variety of illnesses and conditions.

The Spanish found that many of the herbs Aztec healers used were more effective than European medicines. They admired Aztec medicine and were interested in learning from it. The Europeans, however, disliked anything in Aztec medicine that seemed to suggest rituals connected to witchcraft or the devil.

Some herbs the Aztecs used as medicine are still used to help the sick. For example, the Aztecs used catnip to calm patients and catnip tea is sometimes drunk today for the same purpose. Yerba buena, a type of mint, soothed stomach aches. Today it is used to treat aches in the stomach and other parts of the body.

The Aztecs used various parts of the prickly pear cactus to get rid of intestinal worms, strengthen the lungs, and increase mothers' breast milk. Modern scientific studies have shown that parts of this cactus might help control the disease diabetes. The prickly pear may also contain chemicals that can help the body fight other diseases.

Aztecs felt that it was their job to help relieve the suffering of their people. They were not going against the gods in doing so, since the gods had the power to stop the herbs from working. If the gods truly wanted a person to suffer and die, no amount of medicine would provide a cure.

The Aztecs also paid attention to dental health. Diners washed their mouths out with water after eating and picked out any bits of food from between their teeth. The Aztecs had an early form of toothpaste, made out of ashes and honey. The root of a plant served as a brush.

Epilogue

AT ONE TIME, THE AZTECS RULED THE WORLD THAT THEY knew. The Spanish conquest ended the power of the Aztecs and the other indigenous, or native, people of Central and South America. Still, in remote areas, the old ways of life endured. Mestizos—people who were half Spanish and half indigenous—also kept parts of the old culture alive.

MODERN MEXICO

Mexico was a colony of Spain until 1810, when the Mexican people rebelled against their Spanish rulers. After a long war, they won their independence in 1821. However, by then much of the land was owned by wealthy people who were descendants of the original Spanish conquerors. Their estates were called *haciendas,* and the people who worked on them made extremely poor wages.

Poverty and the unfair social structure that kept people of Spanish descent in control fueled many rebellions. In 1910, civil war broke out in Mexico. The war pitted many groups in Mexico against one another, and continued for more than a decade. In 1917, a new Mexican constitution was approved. It ensured that the native peoples of Mexico would have the same rights as people of Spanish descent.

Today, Mexico is a land of opposites. There is great wealth and serious poverty. In 1950, less than half of Mexico's population lived in towns or cities of 2,500 people or more. By 2005, that number had changed dramatically. Today, more than three-fourths of the population live in towns

OPPOSITE
The Plaza of the Three Cultures in Mexico City reflects the Aztec, Spanish, and mixed heritage of the Mexican people. Around the plaza are the ruins of the ancient Aztec city of Tlatelolco, the Spanish Cathedral of Santiago, and the Department of Foreign Affairs building of the Mexican government.

CONNECTIONS

An Aztec Saint

The blending of Aztec and Spanish religious traditions began soon after the Spanish conquest. In 1524, an Aztec farmer was converted to Roman Catholicism by missionaries. They gave him the Spanish name Juan Diego (1474–1548).

On December 9, 1531, Diego was walking from his village to attend mass in Tenochtitlan. As he passed Tepeyac Hill, a woman's voice called him to the top of the hill. There he saw a beautiful young woman dressed like an Aztec princess. She spoke to him in Nahuatl and said she was the Virgin Mary, the mother of Jesus Christ. She asked Diego to tell the local bishop to build a church on that site.

The bishop asked Diego to bring him a sign that proved his vision was real. He returned to Tepeyac Hill. It was the winter, but Diego found Castilian roses (which do not grow in Mexico, but do grow in Spain).

He picked a bunch and brought them to the bishop.

When Diego presented the roses, his cloak fell open and an image of the Virgin Mary was imprinted on it. Soon after, a church was built on the site where she had appeared. It happened to be the same place where there had been an Aztec temple dedicated to Tonantzin, the mother earth goddess. Earlier, the bishop had ordered this temple to be destroyed.

The image is known as the Virgin of Guadalupe, and a very large church called Our Lady of Guadalupe now stands in Mexico City where Diego had his vision.

In 2002, Pope John Paul II (1920–2005), the leader of the Roman Catholic Church, made Juan Diego the first indigenous American saint. During part of the ceremony, the pope spoke in Nahuatl. He also recognized the importance of Aztec culture in Mexican Catholicism.

and cities. The largest city is Mexico City, built on the ruins of the Aztec cities of Tenochtitlan and Tlatelolco.

Within Mexico, poverty and the rights of indigenous people continue to be major issues. The country is a major oil producer and has a ready market for its oil in the United States. Nearly a third of government money comes from the oil industry.

In addition, the North American Free Trade Agreement (NAFTA) opened the Mexican market to major investments. U.S. companies invested more than $148 billion in Mexico, building factories and tourist facilities. Oil and NAFTA have improved the Mexican economy, but the money remains in the hands of the wealthy and poverty continues.

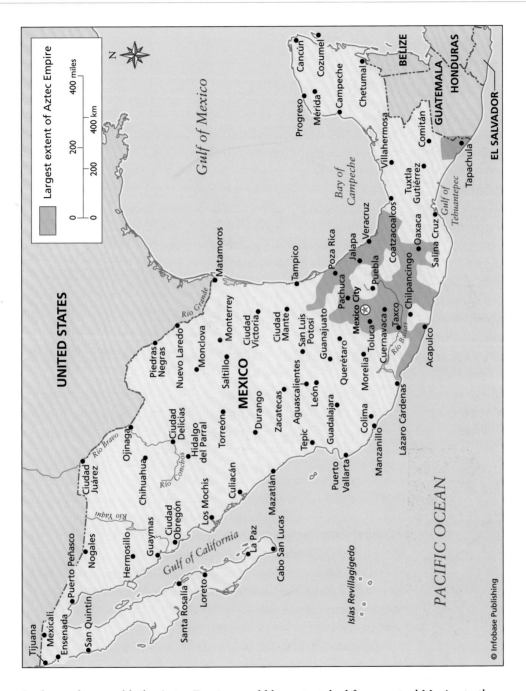

In the modern world, the Aztec Empire would have stretched from central Mexico to the border of Guatemala.

Moving North

Many Mexican people emigrate—legally and illegally—across the northern border and into the United States. They are seeking better jobs. Some small border towns in the north have become almost ghost towns, as the people head for higher wages in the United States. About 8.5 million Mexicans currently live and work in the United States. Their relatives back in Mexico depend heavily on the money they earn and send home to pay for housing, food, clothing, and healthcare.

Half of all Mexicans live in poverty. More than 20 million Mexicans live on less than two dollars a day. One in five suffer from extreme poverty. Often, those in extreme poverty do not have access to fresh water, electricity, or sanitation. In cities, many poor people eat only once or twice a day, and they find their food in garbage bins.

Most poor people live in rural areas. They have little transportation and communication. In some areas, they still do not have electricity or running water. The Mexican government is trying to modernize rural areas, but it takes time. It is difficult to provide education, food, and services to people in remote areas.

Many of the people in these poor rural areas are indigenous people. Their poverty can be traced back to the arrival of the Spanish 500 years ago. At that time, native people were forced onto poor land so that the Spanish could have the best grazing lands for their cattle and sheep.

The indigenous Mexicans face more than just poverty. As young people leave their rural towns for jobs in Mexican factories, the towns have a harder time surviving. The traditional way of life, based on raising maize, is beginning to die. Parents see little reason to teach their children to speak Nahuatl, since the children are moving to larger towns or to the United States.

NATIVE RIGHTS

In 1994, a group of indigenous people began a rebellion against the poverty of native people throughout Mexico. When the fighting was over, more than 150 people had died. The rebel group is called the Zapatista National Liberation Army, named for their hero Emiliano Zapata (1879–1919). During the early 20th century, Zapata fought against the Mexican government. Today's Zapatistas live in the state of Chiapas in the Lacandon rain forest. Chiapas is one of the poorest states in Mexico. The goal of the Zapatistas is to gain land rights and equality for Mexico's indigenous people.

Also during the 1990s, Nahuatl speakers in the Mexican state of Guerrero rose up to defend their rights. People in several towns along the Balsas River joined together to fight the building of a dam that would have destroyed their homes. They won their battle, and the group that led the effort is still fighting for the indigenous people of the area. Unlike the Zapatistas, however, they have used legal means in their struggle, not violence.

In 2001, newly elected Mexican president Vicente Fox (b. 1942) tried to address the concerns of the country's indigenous people. He recommended immediate changes in the Mexican constitution to protect the rights of Nahuatl speakers and others. Mexico's Congress, however, passed a law that did not give the protesters all that they wanted. The new law, for example, made it hard for indigenous people to create their own governments if they had groups who live in more than one state. Mexico's indigenous people still struggle to gain political and economic power.

CONNECTIONS

Art for a Living

Many residents of the Balsas River region make a living by creating art that has become popular around the world. The artists practice *pintura en amate*—"painting in *amate*." *Amate* is a thick paper made from tree bark. The Aztecs used the same kind of paper to make their colorful codices hundreds of years ago.

Today's *amate* painting features scenes of daily life among the Nahuatl speakers of Guerrero. During the fight against the Balsas River dam, the *amate* painters created works that showed the history of the region. A show of these paintings in Mexico City helped bring attention to the people of the region and their struggle to survive.

DIGGING FOR THE PAST

In recent years, archaeologists have uncovered new evidence that has changed the way they think about the Aztecs and their lives. Artifacts found at sites throughout Mexico have influenced people's understanding of Aztec mythology, mathematics, and language. (Artifacts are the artworks and items of daily life left behind by earlier peoples.) Archaeological digs are going on in many places, but some of the most interesting are under Mexico City.

Among the items archaeologists have found is a large stone disk known as the Coyolxauhqui Stone. There is an image of the Aztec moon goddess, Coyolxauhqui, on the disk. The image has an intricately carved headdress with petals, stars, and feathers. According to Aztec mythology, her brother Huitzilopochtli, the sun god, killed Coyolxauhqui by cutting off her head, then pushed her body down the mythical hill of Coatepec ("snake mountain"). The disk shows Coyolxauhqui as her dismembered body rolls down the hill. It was originally placed at the foot of the Huitzliopochtli side of the Great Temple.

Temple in the Subway

There is a perfectly preserved Aztec temple in Mexico City at the subway stop called Pino Suárez. When workers were building the subway, they found a pyramid dedicated to Ehecatl, the Aztec god of wind. They simply built the station around it, leaving the pyramid undisturbed.

The stone was found in the Zócalo district of Mexico City in 1978 by electric company workers who were installing underground cables. Its discovery led to another discovery nearby of the ruins of the Great Temple. The archaeological dig at that site continues. A museum on the site contains the Coyolxauhqui Stone and other items found there.

In 2006, a massive stone slab was put on public display. The slab dates back to 1501. That was 20 years before the fall of the Aztec Empire. It lay hidden beneath the center of modern-day Mexico City for 500 years and was discovered by accident when construction workers readied the site for a new building. The slab is about the size of the average person's living room and is seven feet thick. Archaeologists believe the slab may have been used as an altar for Aztec human sacrifices.

In 2007, two more new finds gave further insight into the Aztecs. Archaeologists made a deep dive into the crater lake of the dormant (not active), snow-covered Nevado de Toluca volcano, 50 miles west of Mexico City. They found some surprising objects: wooden carvings of lightning bolts, cones of incense, and knives made from obsidian. The artifacts were used in rituals to honor the god Tlaloc. Archaeology professor Stanislaw Iwaniszewski of Mexico's National Institute of Anthropology says the lightning bolts were definitely made by the Aztecs and were left more than 500 years ago. "They were left in the lake to bring rain storms. Copal incense was burned to form 'clouds,' and sharp spines from the maguey cactus . . . indicated worshippers brought them there to draw blood from themselves as part of the sacrifice" (quoted in "Aztec Offerings Found in Bottom of Mexico Lake" on Live Science).

An equally exciting find was made three months after the discovery of the lightning bolts. Beneath the Great Temple of Tenochtitlan in Mexico City, archaeologists found a large stone slab carved with a picture of Tlaltecuhtli, one of the Aztec earth goddesses. The goddess is clutching a rabbit in her claw, and the rabbit bears markings for the Aztec year 10 Rabbit, which is 1502. That was the year Aztec *tlatoani* Ahuitzotl died.

So far, archaeologists do not know exactly what they have found. But they believe they may have uncovered the tomb of Ahuitzotl. If they are right, it will be the first burial site of an Aztec *tlatoani* that has been found. In 2007, scientists made radar and sonar surveys

of the earth beneath the slab. The surveys reveal areas that may be rooms within the tomb.

Efforts to uncover the tomb beneath the slab will take many years. The area is prone to flooding because the natural water in the ground is high at the site. Every item found must be examined and catalogued for further study. However, scientists are hopeful. The contents of a royal tomb may reveal information that could unravel many mysteries of the Aztec culture.

DIGGING AT YAUTEPEC

Although most Aztec life centered around Tenochtitlan, that is not the only archaeological site in Mexico. A major dig is under way at Yautepec, another Aztec city in the Mexican state of Morelos. At its height, from about 1430 to 1520, Yautepec was a regional center with four or five smaller cities around it.

Discoveries continue to be made in the ruins of the great Aztec cities. This stone monolith of the Aztec earth god Tlaltecuhtli may mark the tomb of Ahuitzotl.

Motecuhzoma's Pension

In 1550, Spain's King Charles V agreed to pay descendants of Motecuhzoma II a pension (a salary in retirement) equal to 250 ounces of gold a year. The Spanish government paid the money for more than 300 years. When Mexico declared independence, the Mexican government continued to pay, until 1934.

Today, descendants of Motecuhzoma II are demanding that the pension payments be resumed. This would give them a lot of money. Gold prices have risen, and the value of 250 ounces in the 2008 market would be close to $200,000. It is unlikely that the Mexican government will agree to pay this *tlatoani* pension.

Yautepec is more extensively studied because the ruins are easier to get to than they are at Tenochtitlan—which lies under busy Mexico City. Yautepec has three ongoing dig sites: the royal palace, a group of houses, and Yautepec Valley settlements.

The royal palace was something of a surprise. Archaeologists had noticed an earth mound on the outskirts of the city. The modern city of Yautepec was expanding when people realized that new building projects would endanger the Aztec ruins. A team of archaeologists began digging in 1989.

The researchers have uncovered many courtyards, rooms, and hallways built of stone and plaster. Some walls were decorated with murals (wall paintings). After more than 12 years, the archaeologists had uncovered less than one-third of the palace.

The second project includes small homes, piles of garbage, and other areas in the city. The researchers have also dug in present-day schoolyards, church cemeteries, vacant lots, and the backyards of current residents. The researchers found that Yaupetec's Aztecs had many goods that were brought in from other areas. These included obsidian, salt, and pottery. They also owned items made of bronze and copper.

Archaeologists have determined that most of the people in Yautepec were well off. Many worked as artisans or farmers. The city had a large farmers' market at which people could sell the items they made or their surplus fruits and vegetables.

In addition to uncovering new information about how the Aztecs of Yautepec lived, the archaeologists became involved with many Mexican schools. They presented information about Yautepec to more than 1,000 students.

AZTEC YOUTH TODAY

There are few people today who can claim to be pure Aztec descendants. Most have some Spanish ancestors or a mix of Aztec and other indigenous cultures. People with links to the Aztecs take great pride in their heritage.

Nahuatl, the language of the Aztecs, remained in use in the Valley of Mexico, even as people learned Spanish. Today, more than one million people in Mexico speak Nahuatl, and several million more speak other indigenous languages. (Most of these Mexicans speak Spanish as well.)

Most Nahuatl speakers live in central Mexico, in an area surrounding and including Mexico City. The indigenous people of Mexico who speak Nahuatl call their language Mexicano. Many millions of other Mexicans are the descendants of people who used to speak

Many people in Mexico today continue to honor their Aztec heritage. Here they celebrate it with traditional dances.

CONNECTIONS

Mexican Cities

A number of cities in modern Mexico have Nahuatl names. The largest is Mexico City, named after the Mexica people. Here are some of the others.

Acapulco	place of big reeds
Chimalhuacan	place of those who have shields
Cuauhtitlan	place of eagles
Ecatepec	windy hill
Mazatlan	place of deer
Nauhcalpan	place of four houses
Nezahualcoyotl	hungry coyote
Tlalnepantla	middle ground
Tlaxcala	place of tortillas
Xalapa	sandy river
Xochimilco	place of the flowery fields

Nahuatl and were part of the Aztec Empire. Some Mexican-Americans living in the United States also speak Nahuatl or other indigenous languages of Mexico.

Many of those who identify themselves as Aztecs gather to celebrate the culture of their ancestors. They learn how to make clothing in the old way. They learn the songs and rituals of their ancestors. They make traditional clothes by hand. They wear headdresses adorned with feathers. On specific holidays, they gather together and dance Aztec dances.

The dances they perform are private. No tourists or visitors are invited, and none are welcome. The dances recall the Aztecs' love of nature. They honor the basic elements of life: earth, wind, fire, and water.

These Mexican youths look to the traditions and heritage of their past to create a new and positive future. They find that learning the ways of the past provides them with a more stable approach to daily life. Many in the group were once involved with drugs or alcohol. Today, they live a life that is closer to nature and free of many of the problems they faced before. Much of their strength is gained from remembering the ways of the Aztecs.

Time Line

1100	The Aztecs leave their homeland in Aztlan, in northern Mexico.
1195	The Aztecs arrive in the Valley of Mexico, but find little land available to them.
1250	The Aztecs settle on two islands in Lake Texcoco.
1325	The Aztecs found Tenochtitlan as their capital city and the first temple is built. Its sister city, Tlatelolco, is founded soon before or soon after (historians are not sure).
1350	Causeways and canals are built in Tenochtitlan. They connect the island to the mainland and provide transportation in and around Tenochtitlan, which relieves inner city traffic.
1375	Acamapichtli becomes the first Aztec *tlatoani*.
1396	Huitzilihuitl becomes *tlatoani* and forms an alliance with the Tepanecs.
1400	The Tepanecs are defeated and the Aztecs expand their rule over the whole Valley of Mexico.
1427	Itzcoatl becomes *tlatoani*.
1428	The Aztecs join forces with Texcoco and Tlacopan to form the Triple Alliance. They go to battle against the Tepanecas.
1440	Motecuhzoma Ilhuicamina becomes *tlatoani*.
1449	Tenochtitlan is heavily damaged by a flood.
1452–1454	Famine leaves the Aztecs starving.
1454	The rebuilding of the Great Temple begins. The pyramid includes a temple dedicated to Huitzilopochtli.
1469	Axayacatl becomes *tlatoani*.
1472	Nezahualcoyotl, the king of Texcoco, dies. Texcoco is left without a strong ruler and Axayacatl increases his power.
1486	Ahuizotl becomes *tlatoani*.
1487	The Great Temple at Tenochtitlan is dedicated.
1491–1495	The Aztecs expand southward into the territories of Oaxaca and Acapulco.
1502	Motecuhzoma II becomes *tlatoani* of a vast Aztec Empire.
1519	Spanish conquistador Hernán Cortés arrives in Mexico, claims the land for Spain, and meets Motecuhzoma II in Tenochtitlan.

1520	The Spanish imprison Motecuhzoma II. Cuitlahuac is chosen as the new *tlatoani*. Motecuhzoma II dies during a battle between the Aztecs and the Spanish. A smallpox epidemic brought by the Spanish kills many of the Aztecs. Cuauhtemoc becomes *tlatoani* after Cuitlahuac dies.
1521	Cortés and his troops conquer Tenochtitlan and take Cuauhtemoc prisoner.
1522	Tenochtitlan is rebuilt, named Mexico City, and made the capital of the Spanish colony of New Spain.
1525	Cuauhtemoc is executed.
1810	Mexico declares independence from Spain. The Mexican war for independence begins.
1821	Mexico wins its independence from Spain.

GLOSSARY

accountant a person who keeps financial records

adobe a building material made by mixing sand, straw, and water and letting it bake in the sun

alliance a friendship or bond between groups of people

altar an elevated structure, such as a mound or platform, where religious ceremonies are performed or sacrifices are made to the gods or ancestors

archaeologist a scientist who studies ancient people by studying the things they left behind

architecture the way buildings are designed and built; a person who designs buildings is an *architect*

artisan a skilled worker who makes things by hand

artifact an item made by humans, such as pottery or tools, that is later studied by archaeologists

astronomy the study of the stars, planets, and other objects in space

baptism a ritual bathing of a person, often a child

basin an area of land with regions that slope upward

bloodletting spilling one's own blood as part of a ritual

cacao the bean used to make chocolate

calmecac a school for nobles

calpulli a district or neighborhood with shared collective responsibility

causeway a raised road

chinampas small islands the Aztecs built in shallow waters so they could grow crops

city-state a city that functions as a separate kingdom or nation

codex an early form of a book with pages; the plural is *codices*

conquistador the Spanish word for "conqueror"

cremation burning a corpse to ashes

culture the religious, social, and artistic beliefs and customs of a group of people

currency money

dike an earthen wall built to keep out floodwaters

domesticate to raise or cultivate an animal or plant for use in agriculture

dynasty a sequence of rulers from the same family

famine a dangerous shortage of food

fertile able to easily grow (for plants) or have offspring (for animals and people)

fertilizer a chemical substance added to soil to promote plant growth

glyph a character or symbol used in hieroglyphic writing

hunter-gathers people who hunt game animals, fish, and gather wild fruit, roots, nuts, and berries to feed themselves

hieroglyphics a system of writing using individual symbols, called glyphs, to represent words

idol an image of a god that is believed to be sacred

indigenous native to a region

irrigation a system for watering crops

macehualli the commoner class

Mesoamerica meaning "middle America," the area extending from what is today central

Mexico south through modern-day Guatemala and Honduras

mestizo   a person with one Spanish parent and one Native American parent

midwife   a woman whose profession is to help women give birth

missionary   a religious person sent to covert new members to a particular faith

Nahuatl   the language of the Aztec people

noble   a person belonging to a special (and elite) social or political class

nomad   a person with no permanent home who wanders from place to place

obsidian   volcanic glass

patron god   a god who is honored for protecting a particular people, place, or thing

pipiltin   the noble class

plume   a long feather

quetzal   a colorful bird found in Central America

reign   the length of time a particular ruler is in power

ritual   a ceremony carried out according to religious laws and customs

sacred   holy

sacrifice   an offering made to a god

scribe   an official writer, particularly in cultures where writing was not common

shaman   a person who has access to and influence over good and evil spirits

sorcerer   a wizard

steward   the manager of a farm or estate

tlatoani   king or emperor, the word means "he who speaks well"; the plural is *tlatoque*

tribute   something of value paid by one state to another as proof of loyalty or obedience, or to secure peace or protection

BIBLIOGRAPHY

Adams, Richard, E. W., *Prehistoric Mesoamerica*. Norman, Okla.: University of Oklahoma Press, 2005.

Aguilar-Moreno, Manuel, *Handbook to Life in the Aztec World*. New York: Facts On File, 2005.

Aimi, Antonio, *Mesoamérica: Olmecas, Mayas, Aztecas: las grandes civilizaciones del Nuevo Munda*. Madrid: Electa, 2003.

"Artisans and Merchants." The Aztec World, The Field Museum. Available online. URL: http://www.fieldmuseum.org/Aztecs/artisans.asp. Accessed October 17, 2008.

"An Aztec Account of the Conquest of Mexico." Modern History Sourcebook, Fordham University. Available online. URL: http://www.fordham.edu/halsall/mod/Aztecs1.html. Accessed May 22, 2008.

"The Aztec Account of the Spanish Conquest of Mexico." Ambergris Caye. Available online. URL: http://ambergriscaye.com/pages/mayan/Aztec.html. Accessed May 12, 2008.

"The Aztec Empire." The Making of an Empire: The Politics of the Pre-Imperial Kings, Pacific Lutheran University. Available online. URL: http://www.plu.edu/~wilkinam/acamapichtli/home.html. Accessed October 14, 2008

"Aztec Families Demand 16th-Century Pensions." BBC News, August 22, 2003. Available online. URL: http://news.bbc.co.uk/2/hi/business/3172569.stm. Accessed May 22, 2008.

"Aztec, Maya, & Inca Foods and Recipes." The Food Timeline. Available online. URL: http://www.foodtimeline.org/foodmaya.html. Accessed April 14, 2008

"Aztec Music." Aztec-History.com. Available online. URL: http://www.aztec-history.com/aztec-music.html. Accessed April 15, 2008.

"Aztlan and the Origins of the Aztec." Laputan Logic. URL: http://www.laputanlogic.com/articles/2004/12/003-0001-9920.html. Accessed June 3, 2008.

Barclay, Eliza, "Aztec Ruler's Tomb Found Under Mexico City." National Geographic News, August 9, 2007. Available online. URL: http://news.nationalgeographic.com/news/pf/12419282.html. Accessed May 22, 2008.

Bautista, Juan, *Huehuetlatolli*. Translated by Louise M. Burkhart. Personal correspondence, September 25, 2008. From Mexico: M. Ocharte (printer), 1600.

Becerril, J. E., and B. Jiménez, "Potable Water and Sanitation in Tenochtitlan: Aztec Culture." *Water Science and Technology: Water Supply*, Vol. 7, no. 1 (2007). Available online. URL: http://www.iwaponline.com/ws/00701/0147/007010147.pdf. Accessed October 16, 2008.

Bierhorst, John, *Cantares Mexicano: Songs of the Aztec*. Palo Alto, Calif.: Stanford University Press, 1985.

Briggs, Helen, "Oldest New World Writing Found." BBC News, September 14, 2006. Available online. URL: http://news.bbc.co.uk/go/pr/fr/-/2/hi/science/nature/5347080.stm. Accessed May 22, 2008.

Cahill, David, and Blanca Tovías, editors. *New World, First Nations*. Eastborne, U.K.: Sussex Academic Press, 2006.

Carrasco, David, and Eduardo Matos Moctezuma, *Moctezuma's Mexico: Visions of the Aztec World*, Rev. ed. Boulder, Colo.: University of Colorado Press, 2003.

Caskie, Donald M., "Azteca—A Horse Custom-built for Performance, Style, and Tradition." Eqiworld.net. Available online. URL: http://www.equiworld.net/breeds/Azteca/index.htm. Accessed October 21. 2008.

Coe, Michael D., and Rex Koontz, *Mexico: From the Olmecs to the Aztecs,* 5th ed. New York: Thames and Hudson, 2002.

Cortés, Hernán, *Letters from Mexico.* Translated and edited by Anthony Pagden. New Haven, Conn.: Yale University Press, 1986.

Curl, John, translator, *Ancient American Poets.* Tempe, Ariz.: Bilingual Review Press, 2005.

Díaz del Castillo, Bernal, *The Bernal Díaz Chronicle.* Translated and edited by Albert Idell. Garden City, N.Y.: Dolphin Books, 1956.

————, *The Discovery and Conquest of Mexico.* Cambridge, Mass.: Da Capo Press, 2004.

Drye, Willy, "Earliest Mixtec Cremations Found; Show Elite Ate Dog." National Geographic News, April 9, 2008. URL: http://news.nationalgeographic.com/news/2008/04/080409-cremations.html. Accessed May 5, 2008.

Durán, Diego, *Books of the Gods and Rites and the Ancient Calendar.* Translated by Fernando Horcasitas and Doris Heyden. Norman, Okla.: University of Oklahoma Press, 1971.

————, *The History of the Indies of New Spain.* Translated by Doris Heyden. Norman, Okla.: University of Oklahoma Press, 1994.

"The Fall of the Aztecs." *Conquistadors.* Available online. URL: http://www.pbs.org/conquistadors/cortes/cortes_flat.html. Accessed June 22, 2008.

Garibay K., Angel Maria, ed., *Veinte himnos sacros de los Nahuas.* Mexico City: National University of Mexico Press, 1958.

"Geography of Mesoamerica." Heilbrunn Timeline of Art History, The Metropolitan Museum of Art. Available online. URL: http://www.metmuseum.org/toah/hd/m_cam/hd_m_cam.htm. Accessed May 22, 2008.

Gruzinski, Serge, *The Aztecs: Rise and Fall of an Empire.* New York: Harry N. Abrams, 1992.

Guerra, F., "Aztec Medicine." *Medical History,* Vol. 10, no. 4 (October 1966). Available online. URL: http://www.pubmedcentral.nih.gov/articlerender.fcgi?artid=1033639. Accessed October 21, 2008.

Gutierrez, Miguel Angel, "Ancient Pyramid Found in Central Mexico City." Reuters UK, December 28, 2007. Available online. URL: http://uk.reuters.com/article/worldNews/idUKN2742810220071228?rpc=401&=undefined&pageNumber=2&virtualBrandChannel=0&sp=true. Accessed October 16, 2008.

Hamnett, Brian R., *A Concise History of Mexico,* 2nd ed. New York: Cambridge University Press, 2006.

Hassig, Ross, *Aztec Warfare: Imperial Expansion and Political Control.* Norman: University of Oklahoma Press, 1988.

————, *Mexico and the Spanish Conquest.* Norman: University of Oklahoma Press, 2006.

"The Hymn of Huitzilopochtli." *Rig Veda Americanus.* Translated by Daniel G. Brinton. Available online. URL: http://www.sacred-texts.com/nam/aztec/rva/rva01.htm. Accessed October 14, 2008.

Idell, Albert, editor and translator, *The Bernal Díaz Chronicles.* Garden City, N.Y.: Dolphin Books, 1956.

"Indigenous Mexicans Reject New Laws." BBC News, August 15, 2001. Available online. URL: http://news.bbc.co.uk/2/hi/americas/1492124.stm. Accessed May 22, 2008.

Joyce, Stephanie, "The Artistry of Amate." *Americas,* September-October, 2007. Available online. URL: http://findarticles.com/p/articles/mi_go2043/is_/ai_n29419845. Accessed October 21, 2008.

Kessell, John L., *Spain in the Southwest: A Narrative History of Colonial New Mexico, Arizona, Texas, and California.* Norman, Okla.: University of Oklahoma Press, 2002.

Knabb, T. J., editor, *A Scattering of Jades: Stories, Poems, and Prayers of the Aztecs.* Translated by Thelma D. Sullivan. New York: Touchstone Books, 1994.

Koch, Peter O., *The Aztecs, the Conquistadors, and the Making of Mexican Culture.* Jefferson, N.C.: McFarland & Company, 2006.

"Law in Mexico Before the Conquest." The University of Texas at Austin, Tarleton Law Library. Available online. URL: http://tarlton.law.utexas.edu/rare/Aztec/. Accessed May 3, 2008.

León-Portilla, Miguel, *Aztec Thought and Culture.* Norman, Okla.: University of Oklahoma Press, 1963.

———, *The Broken Spears: The Aztec Account of the Conquest of Mexico.* Boston: Beacon Press, 1990.

McNeill, William, Sr., editor, *The Berkshire Encyclopedia of World History*, Vol. 3. Great Barrington, Mass.: Berkshire Publishing Group, 2005. Available online. URL: http://drs.asu.edu/fedora/get/asulib:144831/PDF-1. Accessed October 15, 2008.

"Montezuma's Headdress May Return Home After 500 Years." Bloomberg News, February 9, 2006. Available online. URL: http://www.elginism.com/20060210/322/. Accessed October 20, 2008.

O'Brien, Patrick K., editor, *Oxford Atlas of World History.* New York: Oxford University Press, 1999.

"Pear Cactus Makes Mexican Meals Good for Diabetics," Reuters Health, May 28, 2007. MyDiabetesCentral.com. Available online. URL: http://www.healthcentral.com/diabetes/news-39761-66.html. Accessed October 2. 2008.

Phillips, Charles, *The Aztec and Maya World.* London: Lorenz Books, 2005.

———, *The Mythology of the Aztec & Maya.* London: Southwater, 2006.

Prescott, William Hickling, *History of the Conquest of Mexico.* New York: Modern Library, 1998.

Reagan, Timothy G., *Non-Western Educational Traditions.* New York: Routledge, 2005.

"Recreating the Sound of Aztec 'Whistles of Death.'" CNN.com, June 30, 2008. Available online. URL: http://www.cnn.com/2008/TECH/science/06/30/pre-columbiansounds.ap/index.html Accessed July 3, 2008.

Rubalcaba, Jill, *Empires of the Maya.* New York: Chelsea House, 2009.

Sahagún, Bernardino de, *General History of the Things of New Spain (Florentine Codex).* Translated by Charles E. Dibble and Arthur J. O. Anderson. Reprint. Santa Fe, N.M.: School of American Research and the University of Utah Press, 1979.

San Pedro, Emilio, "Mexico City to Teach Aztec Tongue." BBC News, May 4, 2007. Available online. URL: http://newsvote.bbc.co.uk/2/hi/americas/6621859.stm. Accessed May 22, 2008.

Schwaller, John Frederick, translator, "Broken Bones Littered the Road." Personal correspondence, September 25, 2008.

Smith, Michael E., *The Aztecs.* Boston: Blackwell Publishing, 2003.

———, "Life in the Provinces of the Aztec Empire." *Scientific American*, September 1997. Available online. URL: http://www.wcc.hawaii.edu/facstaff/dagrossa-p/articles/LifeInProvinces.pdf. Accessed October 14, 2008.

———, "Yautepec, An Aztec City." State University of New York-Albany. Available online. URL: http://www.public.asu.edu/~mesmith9/yaucity.html. Accessed May 22, 2008.

Sonneborn, Liz, *The Ancient Aztecs.* Danbury, Conn.: Franklin Watts Library, 2005.

Soustelle, Jacques, *Daily Life of the Aztecs.* Mineola, N.Y.: Dover Publications, 2002.

"Split Imperils Mexican Language." BBC News, November 16, 2007. Available online. URL: http://news.bbc.co.uk/2/hi/also_in_the_news/7097647.stm. Accessed May 22, 2008.

Stacy, Lee, *Mexico and the United States.* Tarrytown, N.Y.: Marshall Cavendish, 2002.

Stevenson, Mark, "Aztec Offerings Found in Bottom of Mexico Lake." LiveScience, May 27, 2007. Available online. URL: www.livescience.com/history/070527_ap_Aztec_artifacts.html. Accessed April 14, 2008.

"Telpochcalli School." Chicago School Alliance. Available online. URL: http://www.chicagoschoolsalliance.org/profiletelpochcalli. Accessed October 16, 2008.

"There Is a Worm in Your Mezcal." Mezcal-de-Oaxaca.com. Available online. URL: http://www.mezcal-de-oaxaca.com/mezcal.htm. Accessed October 20, 2008.

Thompson, Ginger, "Mexico Approves Altered Rights Bill." *New York Times*, April 30, 2001. Reprinted at Center for World Indigenous Studies. Available online. URL: at http://www.cwis.org/fwdp/Americas/zap42001.htm. Accessed October 22, 2008.

Townsend, Camilla, "Burying the White Gods: New Perspectives on the Conquest of Mexico." *The*

American Historical Review, Vol. 108, no. 3 (June 2003). Available online. URL: http://www. historycooperative.org/journals/ahr/108.3/ townsend.html. Accessed October 16. 2008.

Townsend, Richard F., *The Aztecs.* London: Thames and Hudson, 1992.

Tuck, Jim, "The Zapatista Movement—Then and Now." Mexico Connect. Available online. URL: http://mexconnect.com/mex_/zapat1.html. Accessed on May 27, 2008.

"Two Faces of Mexican Music." Library of Congress. Available online. URL: http://www.loc.gov/rr/ perform/concert/0708-mexicanmusic.html. Accessed October 21, 2008.

Van Tuerenhout, Dirk R., *The Aztecs.* Santa Barbara, Calif.: ABC-CLIO, 2005.

"A Woman's Journey." Women in Historic Aztec Society. Available online. URL: http://www.plu. edu/~mumperee/womans-journey/home.html. Accessed May 23, 2008.

FURTHER RESOURCES

BOOKS

Aguilar-Moreno, Manuel, *Handbook to Life in the Aztec World* (New York, Facts On File, 2005)

> This well-illustrated book gathers together the results from recent archaeological discoveries and historical documents. It is organized around central themes, such as the geography of the Aztec world, society and government, religion and mythology, art, architecture, Nahuatl literature, the calendar, industry and trade, daily life, and more.

Carrasco, David, and Scott Sessions, *Daily Life of the Aztecs: People of the Sun and Earth* (Indianapolis: Hackett Publishing, 2008, reprint)

> Two experts on the Aztecs offer a detailed look at Aztec life, including religion, food, arts, and games. The book also examines the conflict between Aztec and European cultures during and after the Spanish conquest and the influence Aztec culture continues to have on modern Mexican society. Many illustrations complement the text.

Díaz del Castillo, Bernal, *The Discovery and Conquest of Mexico* (Cambridge, Mass.: Da Capo Press, 2004)

> This book was written by one of the conquistadors. It gives an eyewitness view of what the Spanish saw and thought when they first encountered the Aztecs and other cultures of Mexico.

Coulter, Laurie, *Ballplayers and Bone Setters: 100 Ancient Aztec and Maya Jobs You Might Have Adored or Abhorred* (Toronto, Canada: Annick Press, 2008)

> The ancient Aztecs, Maya, and other Meso-americans believed that the gods created a world where everyone had a role to play. Some people were born to rule, others to serve. Find out in this book what it was like to be a tax collector, a porter, a pyramid builder, a beekeeper, and a royal cook.

Hall, Eleanor J., *Life Among the Aztecs* (Chicago: Lucent Books, 2004)

> This is a very thorough review of how the Aztecs lived, from the how they wore their hair to how they viewed the world. There are also boxes on specific topics, such as how to pronounce *Nahuatl*, the construction of the *chinampa* gardens that made it possible for the cities to feed themselves, and the works of particular scholars. Well illustrated with drawings and photographs.

Pohl, John, *Aztec, Mixtec and Zapotec Armies* (Oxford, U.K.: Osprey Publishing, 1991)

> The Aztec Empire became the most powerful and feared civilization in the Americas. The Mixtec and Zapotec peoples both formed alliances with and fought many wars against the Aztecs. This work investigates the history, uniforms, and weaponry of the Aztec, Mixtec and Zapotec armies. Original artwork makes it easy to visualize these warriors.

Steele, Philip, Norma Rosso, and Penny Bateman, *The Aztec News* (New York: Walker Books, 2009)

> The lively, unusual format of this book is both factual and entertaining. The *Aztec News* imagines what a news magazine would be like during the Aztec Empire. Feature articles discuss major historical events. Local news talks about festivals and daily life, and there are even advertisements. Special interest coverage includes articles on hunting, marriage, and medicine.

Tucker, Mary, *Mayans and Aztecs: Exploring Ancient Civilizations* (Carthage, Ill.: Teaching & Learning Company, 2002)

Ancient history will come to life as students design a battle uniform based on Aztec thinking, and learn about the diet, work, entertainment, worship, and warfare of these ancient cultures.

DVDS

The Aztec Empire (The History Channel, 2005)

Historians trace the rise of the Aztecs from small group of nomads to the dominant culture of Mesoamerica. The program tours the Great Temple in Tenochtitlan, where ongoing archaeological digs are unraveling some of the mysteries of the Aztecs. It also discusses the continued Aztec influence in Mexico today.

Secrets of the Dead: Aztec Massacre (PBS, 2008)

There was a time when historians believed that the Aztecs viewed the Spanish conquistadors as gods and barely resisted their takeover. But new research has proven that the Aztecs fiercely resisted the Spanish invaders. *Aztec Massacre* looks at this new information and presents a new view of the Aztec response to the Spanish.

WEB SITES

Aztec Ancient Scripts

www.ancientscripts.com/aztec.html

This site looks at the writing system the Aztecs used, including how they wrote numbers. There are many examples of specific glyphs, calendar signs, and place names.

Aztec Calendar

www.azteccalendar.com/azteccalendar.html

This site offers an introduction to the calendars the Aztecs used and how they were used together. Links lead to more information on the Aztec gods. Click on "Calculator," which converts a date in the modern calendar to a date in the Aztec calendar.

Aztec Empire

www.mnsu.edu/emuseum/prehistory/latinamerica/meso/cultures/aztec_empire.html

This is an exhibit in the E-Museum at Minnesota State University. Tour an exhibit that focuses on the archaeology in Mesoamerica, with additional pages on specific archaeological sites, cultures, and technology used by the Aztecs and other Mesoamerican people. Click through links on the calendar, Tenochtitlan, technology and society, and more.

Aztec Math Decoded

news.nationalgeographic.com/news/2008/04/080403-aztec-math.html

This article from National Geographic News describes the special arithmetic the Aztecs developed to measure land and keep track of how much tax was owed.

The Aztecs and the Making of Colonial Mexico

www.newberry.org/Aztecs/index.html

This is a virtual exhibition from the Newberry Library in Chicago that shows original manuscripts, books, and other materials about the Aztecs and their clash with the Spanish. View beautiful pages from their books, maps, pages of Spanish manuscripts, and more.

Aztecs at Mexicolore

www.mexicolore.co.uk/index.php?one=azt&two=aaa

Investigate this Aztec Web site that is designed with kids in mind. The information is fun and fascinating. There are sections on Aztec art and design, artifacts, music, the calendar, the gods, and much more.

The Aztec World

www.fieldmuseum.org/aztecs/

This is an introduction to an exhibition about the Aztecs at the Field Museum in Chicago. The site has a lot of photos of objects from the exhibition, along with information on farmers, artisans, merchants, warriors, rulers, and high priests.

Conquistadors: Mexico

www.pbs.org/opb/conquistadors/mexico/mexico.htm

Learn about the Aztecs and the Spanish conquerors who brought their empire to an end. The site contains information about Aztec culture and how the Spanish reacted to it. Pop-up windows and lots of links make this interesting and easy to navigate.

John Pohl's Mesoamerica

www.famsi.org/research/pohl/index.html

John Pohl is an archaeologist and curator of the Art Museum at Princeton University. His web site features many maps, drawings, and photographs relating to the Aztecs and other Mesoamerican cultures, a history of the Aztecs, and information on many major archaeological sites.

Dr. Michael E. Smith

www.public.asu.edu/~mesmith9/

Dr. Smith is an archaeologist specializing in the Aztecs and a professor at Arizona State University. The site has links to some of Dr. Smith's papers written for a general audience and information on his ongoing research in Mexico.

The Mexica/Aztecs

www.wsu.edu/~dee/CIVAMRCA/AZTECS.HTM

This site from Washington State University is part of a larger project called Civilizations in America. Enjoy an overview of the ancient culture of the Aztec people, including their history, social customs and religion. Also offered is specific information on other peoples of Mesoamerica, such as the Olmecs and Toltecs. A Gallery of American Civilizations includes photographs from the archaeological digs at Tenochtitlan.

Museo Nacional de Antropología

www.mna.inah.gob.mx/muna/mna_ing/intro_ing.html

This is the site of the National Museum of Anthropology (the study of human cultures) in Mexico City. The site has a lot of information in English, including details on all periods of early Mexican history. There are also 3-D images of many items in the museum's collection.

Templo Mayor Museum

http://archaeology.asu.edu/tm/index2.htm

This online museum showcases information on archaeological materials excavated at the Great Temple in Mexico City. The site is divided into eight sections devoted to topics such as the gods, agriculture, trade, and rituals. Click on "Supplementary Pages" and see an A-to-Z guide of the museum's many images. The site also has an excellent glossary.

Picture Credits

INDEX

ABOUT THE AUTHOR

BARBARA A. SOMERVILL is a professional children's nonfiction writer with more than 150 published books. She is the author of *Electrical Circuits, Plant Reproduction*, and several works on recovering animal species, and, under the pseudonym Sophie Lockwood, a series on insects and another on mammals. Somervill is a member of the Society of Children's Book Writers and Illustrators and the North Carolina Writer's Network.

Historical consultant **LOUISE M. BURKHART,** Ph.D., is professor of anthropology at the University at Albany, State University of New York. She is an expert in the Nahuatl language and the 16th-century documentation of Aztec civilization. She is the author of three books and many articles on colonial religion and co-author of four books on Nahuatl theater.